AFFILIATE MARKETING MASTERY

The Ultimate Beginner's Guide to Making Money Online

Marc Jordan

CHAPTER 1: UNDERSTANDING AFFILIATE MARKETING

In this chapter, we embark on a journey into the dynamic world of affiliate marketing. We'll explore the fundamentals of this online business model, dissecting its mechanics and uncovering the remarkable potential it holds for individuals seeking to earn online. From its historical roots to the core principles that drive success, we will lay the groundwork for your journey into the realm of affiliate marketing.

1.1 The World of Affiliate Marketing

In this section, we dive into the captivating world of affiliate marketing, a realm where partnerships, promotions, and profits converge. Here, you will discover the intricate web of connections between affiliates, merchants, and consumers, each playing a unique role in this thriving ecosystem. As we unravel the layers of this marketing strategy, you'll gain a deeper understanding of how affiliate marketing operates and why it has become a cornerstone of the digital economy.

1.1.1 Introduction to Affiliate Marketing

Affiliate marketing, at its core, is a performance-based marketing strategy that has revolutionized the way businesses promote their products or services in the digital age. It stands as a testament to the power of collaboration and innovation in the realm of online commerce.

At its heart, affiliate marketing operates on a simple premise: individuals, known as affiliates, partner with companies to promote their products or services. These affiliates earn commissions for driving traffic or sales to the merchant's website through their marketing efforts. In essence, it's a symbiotic relationship where affiliates benefit from commissions, while merchants gain increased exposure and sales.

The roots of affiliate marketing can be traced back to the early days of e-commerce and the internet's emergence as a commercial platform. It was in the late 1990s and early 2000s that affiliate marketing began to gain traction. Amazon, one of the world's largest online retailers, played a pivotal role in popularizing this marketing model by launching its affiliate program in 1996. This move opened up new avenues for online entrepreneurs and bloggers to monetize their websites by promoting Amazon's extensive product catalog.

Over the years, affiliate marketing has evolved in response to changing consumer behaviors and technological advancements. Today, it encompasses a wide array of promotional methods, from traditional banner ads and product reviews to influencer marketing and social media promotions. The affiliate marketing landscape has become a dynamic and versatile arena where creativity and innovation thrive.

Affiliate marketing's historical context and evolution are intertwined with the internet's own transformation. As the digital realm continues to evolve, so too does affiliate marketing, adapting to new technologies and consumer preferences. It remains an integral part of the digital marketing ecosystem, offering countless opportunities for individuals and businesses to collaborate, grow, and prosper in the ever-expanding online marketplace. In the pages ahead, we will delve deeper into the intricacies of this multifaceted marketing strategy, exploring its benefits, challenges, and the strategies that lead to success in the world of affiliate marketing.

1.1.2 The Affiliate Marketing Ecosystem

In the realm of affiliate marketing, an intricate ecosystem thrives, driven by a harmonious interplay among three primary players: affiliates, merchants, and consumers. Understanding their roles and interactions is fundamental to grasping the dynamics of this vibrant digital marketplace.

Affiliates: The Promoters

Affiliates, often referred to as publishers, are the linchpin of the affiliate marketing ecosystem. They are individuals or entities that partner with merchants to promote their products or services. Affiliates come in a diverse array of forms, including bloggers, content creators, social media influencers, website owners, and email marketers. What unites them is their ability to reach and engage with specific target audiences.

Affiliates leverage various marketing channels and tactics to showcase the merchant's offerings to potential consumers. Their creativity and ingenuity play a pivotal role in crafting compelling content that encourages consumer engagement and, ultimately, conversions. Whether it's through in-depth product reviews, engaging blog posts, informative videos, or enticing social media posts, affiliates act as conduits, directing interested consumers towards the merchant's products or services.

Merchants: The Product Providers

On the other side of the equation, we find the merchants, also known as advertisers or vendors. These are the businesses or individuals that offer products or services, seeking to expand their reach and boost sales. Merchants view affiliate marketing as a valuable means to achieve these objectives without the upfront costs associated with traditional advertising.

Merchants collaborate with affiliates by providing them with unique affiliate links or promotional materials such as banners, product data feeds, or coupon codes. These resources enable affiliates to effectively promote the merchant's products or services to their audiences. When consumers make purchases or take desired actions through these affiliate links, merchants compensate affiliates with commissions, thus establishing a win-win partnership.

Consumers: The End Users

Consumers represent the ultimate beneficiaries of the affiliate marketing ecosystem. They are individuals actively seeking products, services, or information online. Consumers encounter affiliate marketing through the content, recommendations, and promotions created by affiliates.

Within the affiliate marketing framework, consumers have a pivotal role in the value exchange. Affiliates strive to connect consumers with relevant products or services that address their needs or interests. When consumers engage with affiliate content and subsequently make purchases or other valuable actions, they become the driving force behind the affiliate marketing cycle.

The Symbiotic Dance of Affiliate Marketing

The magic of affiliate marketing lies in its symbiotic nature. Affiliates act as trusted intermediaries who connect consumers with merchants' offerings that genuinely fulfill their needs or desires. In return, affiliates earn commissions, providing them with a monetization avenue for their efforts. Merchants benefit from increased visibility, access to new audiences, and, most importantly, incremental sales.

Consumers, while often unaware of the affiliate marketing mechanisms at play, benefit from personalized recommendations and access to valuable content that helps them make informed choices. They receive relevant solutions to their problems or fulfill their desires, all while enjoying a seamless online shopping experience.

In essence, the affiliate marketing ecosystem thrives on the delicate balance of trust and value exchange among affiliates, merchants, and consumers. It's a dynamic and evolving landscape where each player plays a vital role, contributing to the ongoing success of this digital marketing model. As we delve deeper into the chapters ahead, we'll explore the intricacies of affiliate marketing, shedding light on how each player can maximize their contributions and thrive within this vibrant ecosystem.

1.1.3 Why Affiliate Marketing Matters

In an ever-evolving digital landscape, affiliate marketing has emerged as a potent force that shapes the way businesses connect with consumers, drives online sales, and fosters entrepreneurship. Understanding why affiliate marketing matters requires us to delve into its profound significance in the digital economy and recognize its pivotal role in e-commerce and online advertising.

The Significance of Affiliate Marketing in the Digital Economy

Affiliate marketing is a linchpin in the digital economy, serving as a dynamic and adaptable marketing strategy that caters to the changing demands and preferences of online consumers. It operates on a performance-based model, meaning that affiliates are compensated only when their marketing efforts result in tangible actions, such as product purchases or lead generation. This performance-based approach is a significant departure from traditional advertising models, where businesses often pay for ad space without knowing whether it will translate into actual sales.

One of the primary reasons why affiliate marketing matters is its cost-effectiveness. Businesses only incur expenses when affiliates deliver results, making it a financially prudent choice for companies of all sizes. This efficiency is particularly crucial for startups and small businesses with limited marketing budgets, enabling them to compete effectively with larger counterparts.

Affiliate marketing also plays a pivotal role in driving website traffic and customer engagement. Affiliates, often experts in niche markets, curate content that resonates with their audiences. This content acts as a conduit that directs potential customers to the merchant's website, resulting in increased brand exposure and customer acquisition. In essence, affiliates become brand advocates, helping businesses reach audiences they might not have otherwise accessed.

Moreover, affiliate marketing operates within the framework of consent. Consumers willingly engage with affiliate content, seeking information or solutions that align with their interests. This voluntary interaction fosters trust and transparency, as consumers are aware of the affiliate relationship. This stands in contrast to many other forms of digital advertising, where users might encounter intrusive and unwanted ads.

Affiliate Marketing's Role in E-commerce and Online Advertising

In the e-commerce landscape, affiliate marketing is a driving force behind sales and revenue generation. Online retailers leverage affiliates to expand their market reach, tapping into niche audiences that are genuinely interested in their products or services. Affiliates act as digital storefronts, guiding consumers through the purchasing journey and providing valuable insights and recommendations along the way.

Beyond e-commerce, affiliate marketing has transformed the

landscape of online advertising. It has democratized advertising opportunities, allowing individuals and businesses of all sizes to participate in the digital marketing arena. This democratization has fostered entrepreneurship and innovation, as affiliates can experiment with various marketing strategies and niches without the financial risks associated with traditional advertising.

Affiliate marketing also aligns with the modern consumer's preference for authenticity and trust. Affiliates are often seen as relatable figures or subject matter experts within their niches. Consumers value their recommendations, making affiliate marketing an effective means of influencer marketing. In an era where authenticity and credibility are paramount, affiliates bridge the gap between businesses and their target audiences.

In conclusion, affiliate marketing matters because it embodies the digital economy's principles of efficiency, consent, and value exchange. It empowers businesses to connect with engaged consumers, fosters entrepreneurship, and amplifies the reach of e-commerce. As we navigate the intricate landscape of affiliate marketing in the chapters ahead, we will uncover the strategies and insights that enable affiliates, merchants, and consumers to harness its full potential.

1.2 How Affiliate Marketing Operates

In this section, we embark on a journey to demystify the inner workings of affiliate marketing. We will delve into the mechanics that drive this performance-based marketing strategy, unraveling the intricate web of relationships between affiliates, merchants, and consumers. By understanding how affiliate marketing operates, you'll gain invaluable insights into its dynamics and potential for success in the digital realm.

1.2.1 The Affiliate Marketer's Role

Affiliate marketers, often referred to as affiliates or publishers, serve as the driving force behind the affiliate marketing ecosystem. Their roles and responsibilities are pivotal in connecting consumers with products or services offered by merchants. Understanding the multifaceted nature of an affiliate marketer's role sheds light on the intricate web of responsibilities they shoulder and the objectives they strive to achieve.

Responsibilities of Affiliate Marketers

- **Content Creation:** Affiliate marketers are content creators at heart. They craft engaging and informative content that resonates with their target audiences. This content can take various forms, including blog posts, product reviews, video tutorials, social media posts, and email newsletters. The primary objective is to provide valuable information that encourages consumer engagement.
- **Promotion and Distribution:** Affiliates are responsible for promoting the products or services of the merchant they are affiliated with. They strategically place affiliate links or promotional materials within their content to direct potential customers to the merchant's website. This entails selecting the most suitable marketing channels and platforms to maximize reach.
- **Audience Engagement:** Building and nurturing a loyal audience is paramount for affiliate marketers. They engage with their followers, respond to inquiries, and foster a sense of community around their niche. This engagement fosters trust and credibility, making consumers more receptive to affiliate recommendations.
- **Data Analysis:** Affiliate marketers are data-driven decision-makers. They monitor the performance of their promotional efforts meticulously, analyzing

metrics such as click-through rates, conversion rates, and revenue generated. This data-driven approach enables them to refine their strategies and optimize their content for better results.

- **Compliance and Transparency:** Ethical and transparent practices are at the core of successful affiliate marketing. Affiliates must adhere to legal and ethical guidelines, including disclosing their affiliate relationships to their audience. This transparency fosters trust and credibility, which are crucial for long-term success.

Objectives of Affiliate Marketers

- **Generating Sales:** The primary objective of affiliate marketers is to drive sales for the merchants they promote. They earn commissions based on the revenue generated through their affiliate links or promotional efforts. Consequently, their success is intrinsically tied to their ability to convert leads into paying customers.
- **Increasing Brand Exposure:** Affiliates contribute to expanding a merchant's brand exposure. They act as brand advocates, showcasing products or services to their audience. This exposure can lead to increased brand recognition and an expanded customer base.
- **Providing Value:** Beyond sales, affiliate marketers aim to provide value to their audience. They seek to genuinely help their followers by offering solutions to problems, answering questions, and offering valuable insights. By doing so, they establish themselves as trusted sources of information and recommendations.
- **Monetization:** Affiliate marketing provides an avenue for affiliates to monetize their online presence and content. While the primary goal is to generate income through commissions, many affiliates also benefit from monetizing their websites or social media

channels through other means, such as advertising or sponsored content.

In essence, affiliate marketers act as intermediaries between merchants and consumers, bridging the gap by creating content that educates, engages, and influences purchasing decisions. Their ability to balance content creation, promotion, and audience engagement while maintaining ethical and transparent practices is central to their success in the affiliate marketing arena. In the chapters ahead, we will delve deeper into the strategies and tactics that enable affiliate marketers to excel in their multifaceted roles.

1.2.2 Affiliate Tracking and Cookies

Affiliate marketing operates on a foundation of precision and accountability, and at its core lies the intricate world of tracking mechanisms and cookies. These technologies are the invisible threads that connect affiliates, merchants, and consumers while attributing sales and commissions accurately. Understanding how tracking and cookies function in affiliate marketing is pivotal in comprehending the transparency and reliability of this marketing model.

How Tracking Mechanisms Work

At the heart of affiliate marketing's tracking system are tracking mechanisms, which are a set of sophisticated algorithms and protocols that monitor user interactions and attribute them to the correct affiliate. Here's how it works:

1. **Affiliate Link Generation:** When an affiliate partners with a merchant, they receive unique affiliate links or tracking codes. These links are embedded within the affiliate's content, whether it's a blog post, social media post, or email newsletter.
2. **User Clicks on Affiliate Link:** When a user clicks on an affiliate's unique link, they are directed to

the merchant's website. This click is recorded by the tracking mechanism.

3. **Cookie Placement:** Simultaneously, a small piece of data called a cookie is stored on the user's device. This cookie contains information about the affiliate's unique identifier, the merchant's product or service, and sometimes the time of the click.

4. **User Browsing and Purchasing:** As the user explores the merchant's website, the tracking mechanism continues to monitor their activities. If the user makes a purchase or takes a specific desired action, such as signing up for a newsletter, the tracking mechanism attributes this action to the affiliate whose cookie is stored on the user's device.

5. **Commission Attribution:** Based on this attribution, the affiliate is credited with the sale or action, and a commission is awarded accordingly. This process ensures that affiliates are compensated for their role in driving the user to the merchant's website.

The Role of Cookies in Attribution

Cookies play a pivotal role in accurately attributing sales and commissions to affiliates. Here's how cookies come into play:

1. **Cookie Duration:** Cookies have a defined lifespan, typically ranging from a few hours to several months. This duration is set by the merchant and can vary. During this period, if the user returns to the merchant's website and makes a purchase, the cookie ensures that the affiliate still receives credit for the sale, even if the user didn't click the affiliate link again.

2. **Cross-Device and Cross-Browser Tracking:** Some tracking mechanisms employ advanced cookies that can track users across different devices and browsers. This ensures that affiliates receive credit for sales, even

if users switch between their computer, smartphone, or tablet.

3. **Last-Click Attribution:** In many cases, affiliate marketing follows a "last-click attribution" model. This means that the affiliate whose link was the last one clicked before the purchase is credited with the sale. Cookies help in precisely determining this last click, ensuring fair attribution.

4. **Cookie Expiration and Reset:** If a user clears their browser cookies or the cookie expires, the tracking mechanism may lose the ability to attribute a sale to the affiliate. In such cases, if the user revisits the merchant's website through another affiliate's link, the second affiliate may receive credit for subsequent purchases.

In summary, tracking mechanisms and cookies are the backbone of transparency and accountability in affiliate marketing. They enable accurate attribution of sales and commissions to affiliates, ensuring that their efforts are rewarded fairly. While cookies are essential, it's also crucial for affiliates and merchants to communicate clearly about cookie durations and attribution models to maintain trust within the affiliate marketing ecosystem.

1.2.3 Affiliate Networks and Platforms

In the dynamic world of affiliate marketing, affiliate networks and platforms stand as pivotal intermediaries that facilitate seamless connections between affiliates and merchants. They play a central role in simplifying the complexities of affiliate marketing, offering a bridge that enables these key players to collaborate effectively and efficiently. Let's delve into the realm of affiliate networks and platforms, exploring their functions and the critical role they play in this thriving ecosystem.

The Role of Affiliate Networks and Platforms

Affiliate networks and platforms serve as matchmakers in the digital marketing world, bringing together affiliates seeking opportunities to promote products or services with merchants looking to expand their reach. Here's a closer look at their functions:

1. **Aggregator of Affiliate Programs**: Affiliate networks often house a diverse array of affiliate programs from various merchants across different industries. This aggregation simplifies the affiliate marketer's journey, allowing them to access a wide range of products or services to promote within a single platform.

2. **Streamlined Registration**: Affiliates can sign up with affiliate networks or platforms, sparing them the need to register individually with multiple merchants. This streamlined registration process simplifies onboarding, enabling affiliates to begin promoting products more swiftly.

3. **Centralized Tracking and Reporting**: Affiliate networks and platforms typically provide robust tracking and reporting tools. Affiliates can monitor the performance of their campaigns, track clicks, conversions, and commissions earned, all within a centralized dashboard. This transparency empowers affiliates to optimize their strategies effectively.

4. **Payment Processing**: Affiliate networks often handle commission payments. They ensure that affiliates are paid accurately and on time, alleviating the administrative burden for merchants who might otherwise need to manage payments to individual affiliates.

5. **Affiliate Support**: Many affiliate networks offer support and resources to assist affiliates in their marketing efforts. This support can include marketing materials, promotional guidance, and even

educational resources to help affiliates succeed.

6. **Merchant Recruitment:** From the merchant's perspective, affiliate networks and platforms simplify the process of recruiting affiliates. They offer a platform where merchants can present their affiliate programs, making it easier for affiliates to discover and join them.

7. **Trust and Security:** Affiliate networks and platforms often act as intermediaries in ensuring trust and security within the affiliate marketing ecosystem. They establish terms and conditions that affiliates and merchants must adhere to, fostering ethical and transparent practices.

Connecting Affiliates with Merchants

The synergy between affiliates and merchants within affiliate networks and platforms is a testament to the effectiveness of this intermediary model. Here's how they connect these key players:

1. **Affiliate Discovery:** Affiliates browse the affiliate network or platform to discover suitable affiliate programs. They can filter programs based on niche, product type, commission structure, and more. This enables affiliates to find programs aligned with their target audience and expertise.

2. **Application and Approval:** Once an affiliate identifies a program of interest, they apply to join it. The merchant, hosted within the affiliate network or platform, reviews the application and approves or declines it based on various criteria.

3. **Access to Marketing Materials:** Affiliates gain access to marketing materials provided by the merchant. These materials often include banners, product links, and other promotional assets that affiliates can integrate into their content.

4. **Tracking and Attribution:** When affiliates promote products using the provided materials or affiliate links, the tracking mechanisms within the network or platform monitor user interactions. This tracking ensures that any sales or actions resulting from the affiliate's efforts are accurately attributed.

5. **Reporting and Payment:** Affiliates can monitor their performance in real-time through the platform's reporting tools. Once they achieve the minimum payout threshold, the affiliate network or platform processes the commission payment, ensuring that affiliates are duly compensated.

In summary, affiliate networks and platforms serve as vital intermediaries that streamline the affiliate marketing process. They offer a centralized hub where affiliates and merchants can discover each other, collaborate, and benefit from the advantages of a trusted and well-organized ecosystem. This collaborative model not only fosters efficiency but also promotes ethical practices and transparency, ultimately benefiting all parties involved in the affiliate marketing journey.

1.3 The Allure of Affiliate Marketing

In this section, we explore the captivating allure of affiliate marketing, a digital frontier where entrepreneurial aspirations meet the boundless potential of the online world. Affiliate marketing has become a beacon for individuals seeking financial independence, flexible work arrangements, and the opportunity to shape their online destiny. Here, we delve into the multifaceted appeal that draws people into this dynamic realm of digital entrepreneurship.

1.3.1 Advantages of Affiliate Marketing

Affiliate marketing's allure is underpinned by a multitude of advantages that make it an enticing prospect for affiliates. These benefits span financial rewards, flexible work arrangements, and the potential for both passive income and scalability. Let's delve into the advantages that beckon individuals to embark on their affiliate marketing journey:

1. **Lucrative Earning Potential and Low Entry Costs:**
Affiliate marketing offers the potential for substantial income with minimal upfront investment. Commissions based on sales or actions driven by affiliates allow for unlimited earnings as they refine their strategies.

1. **Flexibility and Autonomy with No Product Hassles:**
Affiliates enjoy unmatched flexibility in choosing niches, products, and promotional methods. They can work on their own schedules, and they don't need to create or manage products, focusing solely on promotion.

2. **Passive Income and Scalability with Diverse Revenue Streams:**
Affiliate marketing offers the allure of passive income as affiliate content continues to generate commissions over time. It's scalable, allowing affiliates to expand their reach and diversify revenue sources by promoting products from various merchants within their niche.

In essence, the allure of affiliate marketing lies in its blend of financial potential, flexibility, and the promise of passive income and scalability. Affiliates are drawn to this model for the opportunity it offers to shape their digital destiny and achieve financial independence while exploring their passions and interests.

1.3.2 The Flexibility Factor

One of the defining characteristics that makes affiliate marketing so alluring is its remarkable flexibility and accessibility. It's a digital endeavor that adapts to diverse lifestyles and goals, attracting a wide spectrum of individuals looking for financial independence, meaningful work, and the freedom to chart their own course. In this section, we'll explore the flexibility factor that lies at the core of affiliate marketing's appeal.

Accessibility and Inclusivity

Affiliate marketing welcomes individuals from all walks of life, regardless of their background, location, or resources. Here's how its accessibility sets it apart:

1. **Low Barrier to Entry:** Unlike many traditional businesses that require substantial capital or resources, affiliate marketing offers a remarkably low barrier to entry. With a computer and internet connection, anyone can get started. This inclusivity empowers individuals with limited financial means to participate and thrive.
2. **No Formal Education Requirements:** Affiliate marketing doesn't demand formal education or specialized degrees. It's a merit-based field where success is determined by dedication, creativity, and effective marketing strategies rather than academic qualifications. This levels the playing field for aspiring affiliates.
3. **Global Reach:** The internet's borderless nature means that affiliates can reach audiences worldwide. This global reach transcends geographical limitations, allowing affiliates to connect with consumers from diverse cultures and regions.

Flexibility in Work Arrangements

Affiliate marketing offers a work environment that accommodates a wide range of lifestyles and goals:

1. **Flexible Work Hours:** Affiliates have the freedom to choose when and where they work. Whether it's early mornings, late nights, or during weekends, affiliate marketing fits into a variety of schedules.

2. **Part-Time or Full-Time:** Affiliate marketing can be pursued on a part-time or full-time basis. It's an ideal choice for those looking to supplement their income while working traditional jobs or individuals seeking a full-time entrepreneurial venture.

3. **Remote Work:** Affiliate marketing is location-independent. Affiliates can work from home, coffee shops, co-working spaces, or even while traveling. This flexibility appeals to digital nomads and those seeking a remote lifestyle.

4. **Balancing Family and Work:** For parents and caregivers, affiliate marketing offers the flexibility to balance family responsibilities with income generation. Affiliates can tailor their work hours to suit their family's needs.

Customization to Goals and Interests

Affiliate marketing is highly customizable, allowing individuals to align their efforts with their goals and interests:

1. **Niche Selection:** Affiliates choose niches that resonate with their passions and expertise. This personal connection enhances content quality and engagement with the target audience.

2. **Monetization Strategies:** Affiliates can diversify their revenue streams by selecting various monetization strategies, such as pay-per-sale, pay-per-click, or pay-per-lead models. This adaptability allows them to optimize their income generation.

3. **Scalability:** The scalability of affiliate marketing means that affiliates can tailor their efforts to align with their income goals. As their audience grows, they can expand their promotional activities.

Adapting to Changing Circumstances

Affiliate marketing's adaptability extends to changing life

circumstances:

1. **Career Transition:** It serves as a viable career transition option for individuals seeking new opportunities or experiencing job changes.
2. **Retirement Planning:** Affiliate marketing can be a supplementary source of income for retirees, allowing them to continue pursuing meaningful work.
3. **Side Hustle to Business:** What begins as a side hustle can evolve into a full-fledged online business for those who desire entrepreneurship.

In conclusion, the flexibility factor is a cornerstone of affiliate marketing's allure. Its accessibility, adaptability to diverse lifestyles, and customization to individual goals and interests make it an inviting prospect for those seeking financial independence and a work-life balance that aligns with their unique aspirations. Affiliate marketing truly exemplifies the spirit of the digital age, where opportunities abound for those willing to explore the endless possibilities of the online world.

1.3.3 Success Stories and Case Studies

The allure of affiliate marketing is not just a concept; it's a tangible reality for countless individuals who have transformed their lives through this dynamic online venture. Here, we'll delve into real-world success stories and case studies that illustrate how affiliate marketing has unlocked financial rewards, personal freedom, and the fulfillment of entrepreneurial dreams.

Success Story: Pat Flynn – From Job Loss to Online Empire

Pat Flynn is a shining example of how affiliate marketing can reshape one's destiny. In 2008, Pat lost his job as an architect, thrusting him into an uncertain future. With determination and an entrepreneurial spirit, he ventured into the world of affiliate marketing and online business. Pat's success story is characterized by:

- **Diverse Income Streams:** Pat didn't rely solely on affiliate marketing but diversified his income sources. He combined affiliate commissions with income from his blog, podcast, and digital products, creating a robust online empire.
- **Transparency and Trust:** Pat's commitment to transparency and authentic communication with his audience fostered trust. His audience knew he genuinely believed in the products he promoted, enhancing his credibility as an affiliate marketer.
- **Financial Independence:** Through affiliate marketing and his online ventures, Pat not only achieved financial independence but also inspired countless others through his blog, podcast, and online courses on entrepreneurship.

Case Study: The Wirecutter – Niche Authority and Acquisition by The New York Times

The Wirecutter, a product review website founded by Brian Lam in 2011, showcases the potential of affiliate marketing at scale:

- **Niche Authority:** The Wirecutter focused on in-depth, unbiased product reviews, becoming a trusted resource in the tech and gadget niche. Their content provided valuable insights to readers seeking informed purchasing decisions.
- **Affiliate Partnerships:** The Wirecutter strategically partnered with numerous e-commerce platforms and retailers, earning commissions on products recommended in their reviews.
- **Monetization at Scale:** As their audience grew, so did their affiliate commissions. Their effective monetization strategies caught the attention of media giant The New York Times, which acquired The

Wirecutter in 2016 for an estimated $30 million.

Success Story: Michelle Schroeder-Gardner – Achieving Financial Freedom Through Blogging

Michelle Schroeder-Gardner's journey from financial stress to financial freedom exemplifies the transformative power of affiliate marketing:

- **Personal Finance Blog:** Michelle started her personal finance blog, Making Sense of Cents, to document her quest for financial freedom. She shared her journey to paying off student loans, saving, and investing.
- **Affiliate Income:** Michelle strategically incorporated affiliate links into her blog posts, recommending financial products and services. Her genuine testimonials and financial success stories resonated with her audience, leading to substantial affiliate commissions.
- **Passive Income Streams:** The passive nature of affiliate marketing allowed Michelle to enjoy the fruits of her labor while traveling the world in an RV with her husband. She consistently earns a substantial income from her blog, demonstrating the potential for passive income in affiliate marketing.

Case Study: Amazon Associates – A Global Affiliate Giant

Amazon Associates, the affiliate program of e-commerce giant Amazon, showcases the scale and reach of affiliate marketing:

- **Global Reach:** Amazon Associates operates worldwide, enabling affiliates from diverse locations to promote products on the world's largest e-commerce platform.
- **Diverse Product Catalog:** Affiliates can choose from millions of products to promote, catering to a wide range of niches and interests.
- **Affiliate Success Stories:** Countless individuals and

websites have thrived as Amazon Associates, earning substantial commissions and building profitable online businesses.

In conclusion, these success stories and case studies underscore the transformative potential of affiliate marketing. From achieving financial independence to building online empires and even catching the attention of media giants, affiliate marketing has opened doors to countless individuals seeking financial rewards, personal freedom, and the fulfillment of their entrepreneurial dreams. These stories serve as inspiring testaments to the limitless possibilities within the affiliate marketing landscape.

1.3.4 Potential Challenges and Misconceptions

While affiliate marketing offers a plethora of opportunities and advantages, it's essential to acknowledge the potential challenges that aspiring affiliates may encounter. Additionally, there are certain misconceptions about affiliate marketing that need to be dispelled to set realistic expectations. Let's explore these challenges and misconceptions to ensure a balanced perspective.

Common Challenges in Affiliate Marketing:

1. **Competition:** The affiliate marketing landscape can be highly competitive, especially in popular niches. Affiliates may find themselves vying for the attention of a limited audience.
2. **Constant Learning:** Successful affiliate marketers must stay updated with evolving digital marketing trends, search engine algorithms, and affiliate program policies. The need for continuous learning can be challenging for some.
3. **Content Creation:** Crafting high-quality, engaging content consistently can be time-consuming. Affiliates must invest effort into producing valuable content

that resonates with their target audience.

4. **Uncertain Income:** Affiliate earnings can be inconsistent, especially in the initial stages. Income may fluctuate due to factors like seasonality, changes in affiliate program terms, or shifts in consumer behavior.

5. **Traffic Acquisition:** Generating targeted traffic to affiliate content can be a significant hurdle. Affiliates may need to master various traffic acquisition methods, such as SEO, social media marketing, or paid advertising.

6. **Compliance and Regulations:** Affiliates must adhere to legal and ethical guidelines. Navigating the complex world of compliance, disclosures, and regional regulations can be challenging.

7. **Content Monetization:** While passive income is possible, achieving it requires time and effort. Some affiliates may struggle to monetize their content effectively.

Misconceptions About Affiliate Marketing:

1. **"It's a Get-Rich-Quick Scheme":** Affiliate marketing is not a guaranteed path to quick riches. Success often requires patience, dedication, and consistent effort over time.

2. **"No Initial Effort Required":** Contrary to the misconception that affiliate marketing requires no work, it demands significant upfront effort in building a website, creating content, and establishing an audience.

3. **"Anyone Can Do It Without Skills":** While affiliate marketing is accessible, it does require skills in areas like content creation, SEO, digital marketing, and data analysis. As with any profession, proficiency develops with practice and learning.

4. **"You Can Promote Anything and Succeed":** Effectiveness in affiliate marketing often hinges on promoting products or services that align with an affiliate's niche and audience. Promoting anything and everything rarely leads to success.

5. **"No Investment Needed":** While the initial investment is lower compared to traditional businesses, affiliates may still need to invest in website hosting, tools, and marketing expenses.

Setting Realistic Expectations:

Affiliate marketing can be incredibly rewarding, but it's essential to set realistic expectations:

- **Success Takes Time:** Building a profitable affiliate marketing business typically doesn't happen overnight. It requires consistent effort, learning, and adaptation.
- **Income Variances:** Affiliate income can vary from month to month. It may take time to reach a level of stability and passive income.
- **Learning Curve:** Embrace the learning curve as an opportunity for growth. Continual learning is integral to long-term success.
- **Content Quality Matters:** High-quality, valuable content is key to attracting and retaining an audience. Focus on creating content that genuinely helps your audience.
- **Ethical Practices:** Adhere to ethical affiliate marketing practices, including transparency in affiliate relationships and compliance with legal regulations.

In conclusion, affiliate marketing offers abundant opportunities, but it's not without its challenges and misconceptions. Understanding these challenges, dispelling myths, and setting realistic expectations are crucial steps for aspiring affiliates. With dedication, persistence, and a commitment to ethical practices, affiliate marketing can be a fulfilling and profitable venture.

CHAPTER 2: NICHE SELECTION STRATEGIES

In the intricate world of affiliate marketing, the choice of a niche can significantly influence an affiliate marketer's success. Chapter 2 delves into the art and science of niche selection, exploring the strategies that guide affiliates in picking the perfect niche for their online endeavors. Here, we unravel the essential considerations and techniques that lead to informed niche decisions, setting the foundation for a thriving affiliate marketing journey.

2.1 Picking the Perfect Niche

This section provides a comprehensive guide to the crucial process of selecting an ideal niche for affiliate marketing. Readers will discover strategies for identifying niches that align with their interests, market demand, and profitability potential. By the end of this chapter, they will be well-equipped to make informed niche decisions for a successful affiliate marketing venture.

2.1.1 The Significance of Niche Selection

Niche selection is the foundational step in an affiliate marketer's journey, and its significance cannot be overstated. It serves as the compass that guides an affiliate toward success in the dynamic world of affiliate marketing. In this section, we'll explore why choosing the right niche is critical and how it profoundly influences content creation and audience engagement.

1. Alignment with Passion and Expertise:

Selecting a niche that aligns with your passion and expertise is akin to igniting the spark of enthusiasm in your affiliate marketing journey. When you're genuinely interested in the niche, you're more likely to stay motivated and dedicated to the long-term commitment it requires. Your passion will shine through in your content, resonating with your audience on a personal level.

2. Market Demand and Profitability:

A strategic niche choice involves a delicate balance between personal interest and market demand. While pursuing your passion is essential, assessing the niche's profitability potential is equally crucial. Popular niches with high demand offer more significant income opportunities, as there's a larger audience willing to engage with products or services related to that niche.

3. Content Creation Quality:

The niche you choose fundamentally shapes the content you create. It provides the framework for your articles, blog posts, videos, and social media content. When you're passionate and knowledgeable about the niche, you're more likely to produce high-quality, informative, and engaging content that resonates with your audience. Conversely, attempting to create content in a niche you have no interest in can lead to uninspired, lackluster materials.

4. Audience Engagement and Trust:

Audience engagement is the lifeblood of successful affiliate marketing. A well-chosen niche facilitates deeper connections with your audience. When your content addresses their specific interests and problems, it fosters trust and credibility.

Your audience recognizes you as an authority in your niche, increasing the likelihood of them acting on your recommendations.

5. Competition and Market Saturation:

Different niches have varying levels of competition and market saturation. Overly saturated niches may have fierce competition, making it challenging for newcomers to gain a foothold. Conversely, niches with low competition may offer opportunities for affiliates to establish themselves more easily. Strategic niche selection involves assessing these factors and finding the right balance.

6. Long-Term Viability:

The affiliate marketing journey is a marathon, not a sprint. Your chosen niche should have long-term viability and relevance. Consider whether the niche is likely to endure over time or if it's a fleeting trend. Sustainable niches provide opportunities for consistent growth and income.

7. Diversification Potential:

While your initial focus is on a single niche, consider the potential for diversification within that niche or into related niches. This allows you to expand your affiliate marketing efforts while maintaining a core focus. Diversification can mitigate risks associated with relying solely on one niche.

In summary, niche selection is the cornerstone of affiliate marketing success. It influences your passion, content quality, audience engagement, and income potential. By choosing a niche that strikes a balance between your interests and market demand, you set the stage for a fulfilling and prosperous affiliate marketing journey.

2.1.2 Identifying Your Passions and Interests

Choosing a niche aligned with your passions and interests is not merely a recommendation; it's a strategic advantage in the world of affiliate marketing. This section explores the myriad benefits of selecting a niche that resonates with your personal enthusiasms and provides strategies to help you recognize and leverage your passions effectively.

The Benefits of Passion-Aligned Niche Selection:

1. **Intrinsic Motivation:** When you choose a niche that genuinely interests you, you're inherently motivated to delve deeper into it. Your work becomes a labor of love, and you're more likely to stay committed, even during challenging times.
2. **Authenticity and Authority:** Passion shines through in your content. Your enthusiasm and authentic voice make your recommendations more compelling and trustworthy. Audiences can sense when an affiliate genuinely believes in the products or services they promote.
3. **Endless Content Ideas:** Your passion for a niche often translates into a wealth of content ideas. You'll find yourself naturally curious, continually exploring new angles, and addressing the evolving interests of your audience.
4. **Resilience and Persistence:** Affiliate marketing requires persistence and resilience. When you're passionate about your niche, setbacks become learning opportunities rather than obstacles. You're more likely to adapt and persevere.
5. **Personal Fulfillment:** Beyond financial rewards, working in a niche you love brings personal fulfillment. It allows you to combine your interests with your profession, creating a sense of purpose and satisfaction.

Strategies to Identify Your Passions:

1. **Self-Reflection:** Take time to reflect on your interests, hobbies, and activities that genuinely excite you. What topics do you find yourself reading about, discussing, or exploring in your free time? Identify areas that consistently pique your curiosity.

2. **Problem-Solution Analysis:** Consider the problems or challenges you've encountered in your life. What solutions or products have you found particularly valuable? This can lead you to niches where you have personal experience and knowledge.

3. **Market Research:** Explore potential niches by conducting market research. Look for niches with a balance between personal interest and market demand. Tools like keyword research can help you identify niches with relevant search volume.

4. **Networking and Discussions:** Engage in discussions and forums related to your areas of interest. Interacting with others who share your passions can provide insights and reveal potential niches.

5. **Experimentation:** Sometimes, you may not discover your true passion until you've dabbled in different niches. Don't hesitate to experiment with niche selection and content creation. Your journey may lead you to unexpected and exciting niches.

6. **Audience Feedback:** If you already have an audience or social media following, pay attention to their interests and questions. Your audience's feedback can guide you toward niches and topics that resonate with them.

7. **Consider Future Growth:** While focusing on your current passions is essential, also think about long-term interests and potential niches that may align with your evolving passions.

In conclusion, selecting a niche aligned with your passions and interests is a strategic decision that can propel your affiliate marketing success. It brings intrinsic motivation, authenticity, and endless content ideas to your affiliate marketing journey. By employing these strategies to identify your passions, you'll not only enjoy your work but also connect with your audience on a deeper level, fostering trust and loyalty in your affiliate marketing endeavors.

2.1.3 Evaluating Market Demand

In the intricate process of niche selection for affiliate marketing, understanding and assessing market demand is a pivotal step. This section introduces the concept of market demand and its pivotal role in niche selection. It also provides readers with valuable tools and methods to effectively evaluate the demand for potential niches, ensuring an informed and strategic choice.

The Role of Market Demand in Niche Selection:

Market demand is the driving force behind the profitability and sustainability of an affiliate marketing niche. It represents the level of interest and need consumers have for products or services within a specific niche. Here's why evaluating market demand is crucial:

1. **Income Potential:** Niche markets with high demand typically offer greater income potential. A substantial audience interested in products or services related to your niche can result in higher commissions and more significant earnings.
2. **Audience Engagement:** A niche with strong market demand is more likely to attract an engaged audience. Your content is more likely to resonate with an audience genuinely interested in the niche, leading to increased engagement and trust.
3. **Content Opportunities:** Market demand often translates into a broader range of content opportunities. You'll have a wealth of topics and products to explore and promote, ensuring consistent

content creation.

4. **Sustainability:** Niches with enduring market demand are more likely to remain profitable over the long term. Trends and fads may come and go, but evergreen niches sustain affiliate marketers' income.

Tools and Methods for Assessing Market Demand:

1. **Keyword Research:** Use tools like Google Keyword Planner, SEMrush, or Ahrefs to find relevant keywords and assess their search volume, indicating interest and demand.
2. **Google Trends:** Track search term popularity over time to gauge whether interest in your niche is growing, stable, or declining.
3. **Marketplace & Competitor Analysis:** Analyze online marketplaces and competitors to understand the number of products, customer reviews, and competition levels, indicating demand.
4. **Social Media & Online Communities:** Monitor social media and engage in niche-specific online communities to identify trends, discussions, and engagement levels, providing insights into demand.
5. **Surveys & Industry Reports:** Conduct surveys within your target audience and explore industry reports for data on market trends, consumer behavior, and growth projections, revealing potential demand.
6. **Google AdWords Planner:** Utilize Google AdWords to assess keyword competitiveness and estimated bids, which can indicate strong demand.
7. **Affiliate Program Research:** Investigate the availability and terms of affiliate programs related to your niche, showing demand as merchants are willing to pay for referrals.

In conclusion, assessing market demand is a fundamental aspect of niche selection in affiliate marketing. It's a strategic process that empowers you to make informed choices, ensuring that your chosen niche aligns with both your interests and the interests of a substantial and engaged audience. By utilizing these tools and methods, you can navigate the intricate landscape of market demand and set a strong foundation for your affiliate marketing journey.

2.2 Unearthing Profitable Niches

In the vast landscape of affiliate marketing, discovering niches with untapped potential can be a game-changer. This section delves into the art of unearthing profitable niches, providing readers with strategies to identify opportunities that combine passion and profitability. By the end of this chapter, you'll be equipped to uncover hidden gems within the affiliate marketing realm.

2.2.1 Profit Potential vs. Competition

One of the fundamental challenges in affiliate marketing niche selection is striking the right balance between profit potential and competition. This section explores the delicate equilibrium between these two factors and provides valuable insights on how to identify niches with less competition but high earning potential.

The Balance Between Profit Potential and Competition:

1. **Profit Potential:** Profit potential in a niche refers to the ability to generate substantial income through affiliate commissions. Niches with high profit potential typically involve products or services that command significant market demand and offer attractive affiliate commissions.

2. **Competition:** Competition, on the other hand, is the level of rivalry among affiliate marketers targeting the same niche. Niches with intense competition often have a larger number of affiliates vying for the same

audience's attention and referral commissions.

Insights on Finding Niches with Less Competition but High Earning Potential:

1. **Micro-Niches & Long-Tail Keywords:** Delve into micro-niches and target long-tail keywords to narrow your focus to specific, less competitive areas within your niche. This approach can help you attract a more engaged and relevant audience.

2. **Emerging Trends:** Stay vigilant about emerging trends within your niche, as they often present lucrative opportunities with lower competition. By identifying and capitalizing on these trends early, you can establish a strong presence.

3. **Underserved Audiences:** Recognize and cater to underserved niche segments by tailoring your content and promotional efforts to meet their unique needs. Addressing the unmet needs of a specific audience can set you apart from competitors.

4. **Unique Value Proposition:** Develop a unique value proposition (UVP) that distinguishes your affiliate content from the competition. Highlight what makes your recommendations or content stand out, whether it's in-depth reviews, exclusive discounts, or personalized guidance.

5. **Diversification:** Consider diversifying your affiliate marketing efforts across multiple niches. This strategy reduces your reliance on the success of a single niche and spreads the risk across a broader portfolio.

6. **Local or Regional Niches:** Explore local or regional niches that may have less competition compared to global markets. Localized affiliate marketing can tap into the specific needs and preferences of regional consumers.

7. **Affiliate Program Assessment:** Evaluate the available

affiliate programs within your chosen niche. Look for programs with better commission rates and terms that align with your income goals. A well-structured affiliate program can enhance your earning potential.

8. **Market Research Tools:** Leverage market research tools to gain data-driven insights into competition levels and profitability metrics within potential niches. These tools provide valuable information for making informed decisions.

9. **Continuous Monitoring:** Recognize that niche competition can change over time. Continuously monitor your chosen niche, staying adaptable and ready to adjust your strategies as competition levels and market dynamics evolve. This ongoing vigilance is key to maintaining a competitive edge.

In conclusion, finding niches with less competition but high earning potential is a strategic approach in affiliate marketing. It allows you to carve a niche for yourself and optimize your chances of success. By carefully balancing profit potential, competition, and unique value propositions, you can identify niche opportunities that align with your affiliate marketing goals and set yourself up for a profitable journey.

2.2.2 Trend Analysis and Longevity

In the dynamic world of affiliate marketing, the ability to identify niche trends and assess their long-term sustainability is a skill that can set you on a path to sustained success. This section delves into the significance of understanding niche trends and longevity, offering insights on conducting trend analysis and pinpointing evergreen niches.

The Importance of Niche Trends and Longevity:

1. **Niche Trends:** Niche trends are shifts in consumer preferences, behaviors, and interests within a specific niche. Staying attuned to these trends is vital

because they can influence product demand, consumer engagement, and affiliate marketing strategies.

2. **Long-Term Sustainability:** While capitalizing on niche trends can be profitable, long-term sustainability is equally crucial. Evergreen niches are those that remain relevant and profitable over extended periods, ensuring a stable income source for affiliate marketers.

How to Conduct Trend Analysis and Identify Evergreen Niches:

1. **Industry Reports & Google Trends:** Start by exploring industry-specific reports and publications. These often provide valuable insights into emerging trends, market growth projections, and consumer behavior. Additionally, use Google Trends to track the popularity of search terms related to your niche over time. Look for consistent or growing interest in these terms as an indicator of an evergreen niche.

2. **Social Media & Forums:** Keep an eye on social media platforms and niche-specific forums. They can offer real-time insights into trending topics and discussions within your chosen niche. Look for recurring hashtags and viral content, and assess whether these trends have the potential to endure.

3. **Keyword Research:** Conduct thorough keyword research to identify niche-related keywords. Pay close attention to keywords with a stable or upward trend in search volume. Avoid niches with keywords that exhibit a sharp decline in interest, as this could indicate an unsustainable trend.

4. **Product Lifecycle:** Examine the product lifecycle within your chosen niche. Are there new product releases or updates that suggest ongoing consumer interest? Evergreen niches often feature products with

enduring appeal, so keep an eye out for such signs of longevity.

5. **Historical Data:** Study historical data and trends within your niche. Look for consistent patterns of demand or seasonal fluctuations. Understanding past trends can provide valuable insights into future niche sustainability.

6. **Audience Feedback:** Engage with your target audience to gather feedback on their evolving needs and preferences. Conduct surveys or polls to gain a deeper understanding of their pain points and interests. This audience feedback can guide your content and product promotion strategies.

7. **Competition Analysis:** Analyze the competitive landscape within your niche. Evergreen niches tend to have established competitors who have been operating successfully for an extended period. High competition turnover may indicate niche instability, so look for niches with consistent competition.

8. **Diversification:** Consider diversifying your affiliate marketing efforts across niches with varying trend profiles. Combining trending niches with evergreen niches can provide a balance between short-term gains and long-term stability in your affiliate portfolio.

9. **Continuous Monitoring:** Recognize that niche trends can evolve rapidly. Continuously monitor your chosen niche for shifts in consumer behavior and preferences. Be prepared to adapt your content and strategies accordingly to maintain relevance in the ever-changing landscape of affiliate marketing.

In summary, conducting trend analysis and identifying evergreen niches is a dynamic process that involves ongoing research and adaptability. By staying informed about niche trends and assessing their potential longevity, you can make informed niche selection decisions and build a sustainable affiliate marketing business that withstands the test of time.

2.2.3 Affiliate Programs Availability

In the pursuit of unearthing profitable niches for affiliate marketing, the availability of suitable affiliate programs is a critical factor to consider. This section underlines the significance of affiliate programs in niche selection and offers comprehensive guidance on researching the availability of affiliate programs within a chosen niche.

The Relevance of Affiliate Programs in Niche Selection:

Affiliate programs serve as the backbone of affiliate marketing. They are agreements between merchants or product/service providers and affiliates. These programs define the terms, commissions, and tracking mechanisms that facilitate affiliate marketing partnerships. The availability and suitability of affiliate programs directly impact your niche selection for several reasons:

1. **Income Source:** Affiliate programs are the primary source of income for affiliate marketers. Your ability to earn commissions is contingent upon the existence of affiliate programs within your chosen niche.
2. **Product Promotion:** Affiliate programs determine which products or services you can promote and earn commissions from. An absence of relevant affiliate programs can limit your promotional opportunities.
3. **Commission Rates:** Different affiliate programs offer varying commission rates. The availability of programs with competitive commission structures can significantly influence your earning potential.
4. **Tracking and Reporting:** Affiliate programs provide tracking tools and reporting mechanisms that allow you to monitor your performance and earnings. The quality of these tools can affect your ability to optimize your affiliate marketing strategies.

Guidance on Researching Affiliate Programs Availability:

1. **Niche Research:** Start your journey with thorough niche research to identify products or services that resonate with your audience. Understanding your niche guides your search for relevant affiliate programs tailored to your audience's needs.

2. **Search Engines:** Leverage search engines to find affiliate programs related to your niche. Utilize search queries like "[Niche] affiliate programs" or "[Product/Service] affiliate programs" to explore search results and relevant websites.

3. **Affiliate Networks:** Explore established affiliate networks like ShareASale and CJ Affiliate. These platforms offer a wide variety of niche-specific programs, simplifying the search for affiliates that align with your niche.

4. **Merchant Websites:** Visit the websites of potential merchants within your niche. Look for sections labeled "Affiliate Program" or "Partnerships" as many merchants offer affiliate programs directly to affiliates.

5. **Directories:** Utilize affiliate program directories such as AffiliatePrograms.com and AffiliateSeeking.com. These platforms provide searchable lists of programs across different niches, streamlining your search efforts.

6. **Competitor Analysis:** Analyze your niche competitors and the affiliate programs they promote. This analysis can provide valuable insights into which programs are active and relevant within your niche.

7. **Aggregator Platforms:** Consider using affiliate program aggregator platforms like AffScanner or OfferVault. These platforms compile affiliate programs from various niches, simplifying your search for relevant options.

8. **Reviews and Feedback:** Read reviews and feedback from fellow affiliates who have experience with specific programs. This can help you assess program reputation, reliability, and commission structures.

9. **Contact Program Managers:** Reach out to program managers or contact points listed on affiliate program websites. Engage in conversations to inquire about program suitability for your niche and the terms they offer for affiliates.

In conclusion, the availability of affiliate programs is a pivotal factor in niche selection for affiliate marketing. Thorough research and diligence in identifying and evaluating relevant affiliate programs within your chosen niche are essential for building a successful and profitable affiliate marketing business.

2.3 Mastering Niche Research

Niche research is the compass that guides affiliate marketers toward profitable opportunities. In this section, we delve into the essential art of mastering niche research. Here, you will learn the strategies, techniques, and tools necessary to uncover valuable insights, understand your audience, and make informed decisions that pave the way for a successful affiliate marketing journey.

2.3.1 Competitor Analysis

Competitor analysis is a fundamental aspect of niche research that offers invaluable insights to affiliate marketers. In this section, we explore the benefits of competitor analysis in niche research and provide a step-by-step process for effectively analyzing competitors and identifying gaps within your chosen niche.

The Benefits of Competitor Analysis in Niche Research:

1. **Informed Decision-Making:** Competitor analysis

provides critical data and insights that enable you to make informed decisions about your niche strategy. It helps you understand the competitive landscape and identify opportunities.

2. **Identifying Market Trends:** By studying competitors, you can uncover emerging market trends, consumer preferences, and successful strategies. This information allows you to align your efforts with the direction of the niche.

3. **Gap Identification:** Competitor analysis reveals gaps and areas where competitors may be underperforming or neglecting. These gaps present opportunities for you to offer unique value to your audience.

4. **Audience Insights:** Understanding your competitors also means gaining insights into their audience. You can learn about their demographics, preferences, and pain points, which can inform your content and promotional strategies.

5. **Optimizing Your Approach:** By observing both successful and unsuccessful tactics used by competitors, you can optimize your affiliate marketing approach. You can replicate what works and avoid pitfalls.

Step-by-Step Process for Competitor Analysis:

1. **Identify Competitors:** Begin by identifying your competitors within your chosen niche. Utilize search engines, niche-specific directories, and social media platforms to discover websites and affiliates operating in your niche. This initial step lays the groundwork for understanding your competitive landscape.

2. **Content Evaluation:** Conduct a thorough evaluation of the content produced by your competitors. This evaluation should encompass various content types, including blog posts, videos, podcasts, and

social media content. Assess the quality, depth, and engagement of their content to gain insights into their strategies and tactics.

3. **Keyword and SEO Analysis:** Delve into your competitors' keyword and SEO strategies to uncover valuable insights. Utilize SEO tools to identify the keywords your competitors are targeting and assess their on-page SEO efforts. Understanding their SEO approach helps you identify opportunities to improve your own website's visibility and ranking.

4. **Backlink Assessment:**Investigate the backlinks pointing to your competitors' websites to gauge their backlink profile's quality and quantity. Backlink analysis tools can assist in this task by providing data on the sources of their backlinks. Assessing backlinks helps you understand how authoritative and credible their online presence is.

5. **Social Media Presence:** Scrutinize your competitors' social media presence across various platforms, considering the platforms they use, the frequency of their posts, and the level of engagement they maintain. Understanding their social media strategy can guide your own efforts to build a strong online presence and connect with your audience effectively.

6. **Monetization Methods:** Research how your competitors monetize their affiliate marketing efforts, including whether they primarily use banner ads, affiliate links, email marketing, or other methods. Analyzing their approach to revenue generation provides insights into successful monetization strategies within your niche.

7. **Audience Engagement:** Evaluate how competitors engage with their audience by examining interactions such as comments, likes, shares, and responses to inquiries. This assessment helps gauge the level of community engagement they maintain and the

effectiveness of their communication.

8. **Identifying Opportunities:** Based on your comprehensive analysis of competitors, pinpoint areas where they may be falling short or neglecting. These gaps represent opportunities for you to differentiate yourself and provide unique value to your audience.

9. **Continuous Monitoring:** Competitor analysis is not a one-time task; it's an ongoing process. Continuously monitor your competitors to stay updated on their strategies and any changes in the niche landscape. This continuous monitoring ensures that you remain competitive and relevant within your niche.

In conclusion, competitor analysis is a powerful tool in niche research, providing you with insights that inform your affiliate marketing strategy. By following a systematic approach to analyzing your competitors and identifying gaps, you can position yourself for success within your chosen niche.

2.3.2 Keyword Research

Keyword research is a cornerstone of niche exploration in affiliate marketing, offering valuable insights into what your target audience is searching for online. In this section, we introduce keyword research as an essential tool for niche exploration and provide strategies for finding relevant keywords and assessing their potential within your chosen niche.

Introducing Keyword Research as a Valuable Tool:

Keyword research is the process of identifying the specific words and phrases (keywords) that people use when searching for information, products, or services online. In the context of niche exploration, keyword research serves several critical purposes:

1. **Understanding Audience Intent:** Keyword research

reveals the questions, problems, and interests of your target audience. It helps you align your content with their intent.

2. **Content Ideas:** Keywords provide a wealth of content ideas. They guide your content creation process by highlighting the topics and subjects your audience cares about.

3. **SEO Optimization:** Optimizing your content for relevant keywords improves your website's visibility in search engine results. This increases the chances of attracting organic traffic.

4. **Competitive Analysis:** By analyzing keywords used by competitors, you can gain insights into their content strategy and audience engagement.

Strategies for Finding Relevant Keywords and Assessing Their Potential:

1. **Brainstorm and Mind Map:** Start by brainstorming broad topics related to your niche and create a mind map or list of keywords representing these themes. This initial step helps you outline the core subjects within your niche.

2. **Google Tools:** Utilize Google's autocomplete feature and explore the "Related Searches" at the bottom of search results to discover popular queries related to your niche. These suggestions can provide valuable keyword ideas directly from search engine users.

3. **Keyword Research Tools:** Leverage keyword research tools such as Google Keyword Planner, SEMrush, Ahrefs, or Moz Keyword Explorer to access data on search volume, competition, and related keywords. These tools help you analyze keyword potential with comprehensive insights.

4. **Long-Tail Keywords:** Identify long-tail keywords by thinking about specific user questions and needs

within your niche. These longer, more specific phrases often reflect higher user intent and can be valuable for targeting a focused audience.

5. **Competitor Analysis:** Analyze your competitors' content to uncover the keywords they are targeting. This competitive research can reveal keywords that resonate with your niche audience and guide your keyword selection.

6. **Forums and Q&A Sites:** Explore niche-specific forums like Reddit and Quora, along with discussion boards, to discover frequently asked questions and common topics. These platforms are excellent sources of keyword inspiration based on real user queries.

7. **Social Media Monitoring:** Monitor relevant social media platforms and pay attention to trending topics and popular hashtags within your niche. These trends can serve as keyword inspiration and offer insights into ongoing discussions.

8. **Trend Analysis:** Stay updated on niche trends using tools like Google Trends to identify rising search queries. Trends can influence keyword popularity, helping you align your content with current interests.

9. **Keyword Difficulty Assessment:** Assess keyword difficulty and competition levels for your chosen keywords using research tools. Aim for keywords that strike a balance between relevance to your niche and manageable competition, ensuring your content can rank effectively.

In conclusion, keyword research is a foundational aspect of niche exploration in affiliate marketing. By employing these strategies to find relevant keywords and assess their potential, you can uncover valuable insights into your niche, create targeted content, and optimize your affiliate marketing efforts for maximum visibility and audience engagement.

2.3.3 Audience Persona Development

Understanding your target audience is paramount in affiliate marketing, and the process of audience persona development is key to achieving this understanding. In this section, we stress the importance of comprehending your audience and share techniques for creating detailed audience personas that allow you to tailor your content effectively.

Stressing the Importance of Understanding the Target Audience:

1. **Relevance:** Knowing your audience enables you to create content and affiliate promotions that are highly relevant to their needs, interests, and pain points.
2. **Engagement:** Tailoring your content to your audience increases engagement and trust. When visitors feel that your content speaks directly to them, they are more likely to convert.
3. **Content Strategy:** Audience understanding informs your content strategy, helping you choose topics, formats, and communication channels that resonate with your audience.
4. **Product Promotion:** Knowing your audience's preferences allows you to select affiliate products or services that align with their needs, increasing the likelihood of conversions.

Techniques for Creating Detailed Audience Personas:

1. **Demographic and Psychographic Insights:** Collect both basic demographic data (age, gender, location) and dive deeper into psychographics (lifestyle, values, interests) to understand your audience's motivations and behaviors.
2. **Pain Points and Goals:** Identify the specific challenges and pain points your audience faces within your niche.

Additionally, understand their goals and aspirations related to your niche.

3. **Content Preferences and Channels:** Determine your audience's content format preferences (articles, videos, podcasts) and communication channels (social media, forums). Be present where your audience is active and tailor content accordingly.

4. **Keyword and Search Behavior:** Analyze your audience's keyword search behavior to uncover their questions and interests. This data informs your content strategy and helps you address their needs effectively.

5. **Feedback and Competitor Analysis:** Gather feedback from your audience and study the audience of your niche competitors. This real-time data and competitor insights provide valuable guidance for audience persona development.

6. **Create Personas and Use Cases:** Based on the collected data, create detailed audience personas, each representing a segment of your audience with unique characteristics and needs. Develop use cases that illustrate how these personas interact with your content and promotions.

7. **Continuous Monitoring and Adaptation:** Remember that audience personas are not static. Continuously monitor and update them as your niche and audience evolve over time to ensure your strategies remain relevant.

In conclusion, audience persona development is a pivotal step in niche exploration for affiliate marketing. By investing time and effort in understanding your target audience and creating detailed personas, you can tailor your content, promotions, and strategies to effectively address their specific needs and preferences. This, in turn, enhances engagement, builds trust, and increases the likelihood of affiliate marketing success.

2.3.4 Testing and Validation

Niche research is an iterative process that involves exploration, assessment, and refinement. In this section, we delve into the importance of recognizing the iterative nature of niche research and provide insights on how to test and validate chosen niches before making a full-scale commitment.

The Iterative Nature of Niche Research:

1. **Continuous Learning:** Niche research is not a one-time task; it's an ongoing journey. As an affiliate marketer, you're continuously learning about your niche, audience, and the evolving market landscape.
2. **Adaptability:** Market conditions change, audience preferences evolve, and new opportunities arise. Embracing the iterative nature of niche research allows you to adapt to these changes and stay relevant.
3. **Optimization:** Iteration allows you to optimize your affiliate marketing strategies based on data and feedback. You can refine your content, promotional tactics, and product selection to improve results.

How to Test and Validate Chosen Niches:

1. **Preliminary Research and Market Demand:** Begin with preliminary research to identify potential niches, focusing on market demand, competition, and profitability indicators.
2. **Prototype Content and Engagement Metrics:** Develop prototype content and closely monitor engagement metrics like views, likes, shares, comments, and click-through rates. Positive engagement indicates audience interest.
3. **Gather Feedback and Conversion Rates:** Encourage audience feedback on prototype content and analyze conversion rates if promoting affiliate products. Understanding what resonates and drives conversions

is crucial.

4. **Competitor Analysis and Benchmarking:** Benchmark your niche strategies against successful competitors in the chosen niche to evaluate your performance relative to industry leaders.

5. **A/B Testing and Keyword Performance:** Conduct A/B testing to optimize content elements and assess keyword performance, ensuring your pages rank well and attract organic traffic.

6. **Audience Surveys and Community Engagement:** If feasible, conduct surveys to gather direct feedback and engage with niche-specific communities to validate your niche choice through discussions and insights.

7. **Gradual Scaling and Trend Monitoring:** Gradually scale your efforts within validated niches and stay vigilant for changes in trends and audience behavior, adjusting strategies accordingly.

8. **Strategic Diversification and Periodic Review:** Consider diversifying into related sub-niches strategically and review niche performance periodically, remaining open to pivoting or refining strategies based on ongoing data and insights.

In conclusion, testing and validating chosen niches are vital steps in the niche research process. By embracing the iterative nature of niche exploration and using data-driven validation methods, you can minimize risks and increase the chances of success in your affiliate marketing endeavors. Continuously adapt and optimize your strategies based on feedback and evolving market conditions to thrive in your chosen niche.

CHAPTER 3: EXPLORING AFFILIATE PROGRAMS

In the journey of affiliate marketing, Chapter 3 explores the essential step of exploring affiliate programs. This chapter delves into the world of affiliate programs, serving as a guide for affiliate marketers seeking to find, select, and engage with programs that align with their niche and objectives. Here, we unravel the intricacies of scouting for affiliate programs, selecting prime affiliate partnerships, and mastering the art of negotiating commissions.

3.1 Scouting for Affiliate Programs

Scouting for affiliate programs is a pivotal phase in an affiliate marketer's journey, dedicated to unraveling the intricacies of discovering and evaluating affiliate programs that resonate with your niche, goals, and audience. By the end of this section, you'll be equipped with the knowledge and strategies needed to identify prime affiliate partnerships that can drive your affiliate marketing success.

3.1.1 The Importance of Diverse Affiliate Programs

Affiliate marketers often hear the adage "don't put all your eggs in one basket." This wisdom holds true in the affiliate marketing world, where diversifying your affiliate programs can significantly impact your success. In this section, we delve into the importance of diversifying affiliate programs and the benefits it brings, including reduced risk and enhanced income potential.

Benefits of Diversifying Affiliate Programs:

1. **Reduced Risk:** Diversification is a risk management strategy. By spreading your efforts across multiple affiliate programs, you reduce the risk of relying too heavily on one source of income. If a single program experiences a downturn or changes its terms, your overall income remains more stable.

2. **Enhanced Income Potential:** Diversifying allows you to tap into different income streams. Each affiliate program offers unique products, services, and commission structures. This variety can lead to a more robust and diversified income portfolio.

3. **Adaptation to Market Changes:** Affiliate marketing landscapes are dynamic. Markets can change, products can become outdated, and consumer preferences evolve. Diverse affiliate programs provide flexibility to adapt to these changes by shifting focus to more profitable opportunities.

4. **Exploration of Niche Variations:** Some niches have variations or sub-niches that cater to specific audience segments. Diversifying allows you to explore these variations and identify which sub-niches perform best for your audience.

5. **Access to Different Audiences:** Each affiliate program may have its own customer base and target audience. Diversification gives you access to a wider range of potential customers, allowing you to expand your reach.

6. **Mitigation of Dependency:** Relying solely on one affiliate program can create dependency. Diversification ensures you're not entirely dependent

on the decisions and stability of a single program or merchant.

Strategies for Diversifying Affiliate Programs:

1. **Choose Complementary Programs:** Look for affiliate programs that complement each other within your niche. For example, if you promote fitness products, you can diversify with programs offering workout equipment, supplements, and online fitness courses.
2. **Explore Different Niches:** Consider exploring related niches that align with your audience's interests. Expanding into complementary niches can diversify your income while staying relevant to your audience.
3. **Mix High and Low Commissions:** Balance high-commission programs with those that offer lower but steady commissions. High-commission programs can provide quick wins, while lower-commission programs offer long-term stability.
4. **Consider Affiliate Networks:** Affiliate networks often host a variety of programs across different niches. Joining such networks provides access to a diverse range of affiliate programs in one place.
5. **Monitor Performance:** Continuously monitor the performance of your affiliate programs. Identify which programs are generating the most income and which may need optimization or replacement.
6. **Test and Experiment:** Don't be afraid to experiment with new affiliate programs to see how they perform. Testing allows you to identify the most lucrative opportunities.
7. **Review Program Terms:** Carefully review the terms and conditions of each affiliate program. Ensure they align with your goals and expectations, and be aware of any exclusivity clauses that may limit your ability to diversify.

In conclusion, diversifying affiliate programs is a strategic move that can reduce risk and enhance your income potential as an affiliate marketer. By spreading your efforts across multiple programs, you can adapt to changing market conditions, explore new niches, and access a wider range of audiences, ultimately increasing your chances of long-term success in the affiliate marketing landscape.

3.1.2 Where to Find Affiliate Programs

Finding the right affiliate programs to partner with is a crucial step in your affiliate marketing journey. In this section, we explore various sources and platforms where you can discover affiliate programs. We'll provide insights into online directories, affiliate networks, and individual company websites to help you identify the best affiliate partnerships for your niche and goals.

Online Directories for Affiliate Programs:

1. **Affiliate Program Directories:** Several online directories are dedicated to listing affiliate programs across various niches. Some popular directories include:
   a. AffiliatePrograms.com
   b. AssociatePrograms.com
   c. AffiliateSeeking.com
   d. OfferVault.com
   e. AffiBank.com

2. **Niche-Specific Directories:** Depending on your niche, you may find directories tailored to specific industries or interests. These directories often curate programs relevant to your audience.

3. **Affiliate Marketing Forums:** Online forums like Warrior Forum and Digital Point have sections where affiliates discuss and share affiliate programs they've had success with. These forums can be valuable for

discovering lesser-known programs.

Affiliate Networks:

1. **Major Affiliate Networks:** Large affiliate networks host a wide range of affiliate programs from various industries. Some well-known affiliate networks include:
   a. ClickBank
   b. ShareASale
   c. CJ Affiliate (formerly Commission Junction)
   d. Rakuten Advertising (formerly Rakuten Marketing)
2. **Niche-Specific Networks:** Some affiliate networks specialize in specific niches, such as health and wellness, technology, or fashion. These networks can provide tailored opportunities.
3. **Local Affiliate Networks:** Depending on your target audience's location, consider exploring local or regional affiliate networks that offer programs specific to certain countries or regions.

Individual Company Websites:

1. **Product or Service Providers:** If you have specific companies or brands in mind that you'd like to promote, visit their official websites. Many businesses have affiliate programs, often listed under "Affiliates," "Partners," or "Join Our Team" sections.
2. **Marketplace Websites:** Platforms like Amazon Associates allow you to become an affiliate directly through their website. Look for major online retailers or marketplace websites that offer affiliate programs.
3. **Software and SaaS Companies:** Companies offering software or Software as a Service (SaaS) products frequently have affiliate programs. Check the websites of popular software providers within your niche.

Search Engines:

1. **Google Search:** Utilize search engines to discover affiliate programs. Use relevant keywords, such as "affiliate program for [your niche]" or "[product/service] affiliate program."
2. **Bing and Yahoo:** Don't limit your searches to Google alone. Bing and Yahoo can yield different results and lead you to lesser-known programs.

Social Media and Groups:

1. **LinkedIn:** Join LinkedIn groups related to affiliate marketing or your niche. Affiliates often share insights and affiliate program recommendations within these groups.
2. **Facebook and Twitter:** Search for relevant hashtags and groups on Facebook and Twitter. You may come across affiliate marketers discussing programs and sharing opportunities.

Affiliate Program Aggregators:

Affiliate Program Aggregator Websites: Some websites aggregate affiliate programs from various sources and present them in a searchable database. These platforms can be convenient for affiliate program discovery.

When searching for affiliate programs, keep the following tips in mind:

- **Read Program Terms:** Carefully review the terms and conditions of each program to ensure they align with your goals and expectations.
- **Consider Your Audience:** Choose programs that align with the interests and needs of your target audience. Programs that resonate with your audience are more likely to convert.

- **Track Record:** Research the reputation and track record of the affiliate program or network. Look for reviews and testimonials from other affiliates.
- **Evaluate Commission Structures:** Compare commission rates, payment methods, and frequency to determine the potential income from each program.
- **Stay Updated:** Affiliate programs may change or close, so it's essential to regularly check and update your program selection.

In conclusion, discovering affiliate programs involves exploring various sources, from online directories and affiliate networks to individual company websites and social media platforms. By casting a wide net and conducting thorough research, you can identify affiliate programs that align with your niche and audience, setting the stage for successful affiliate marketing partnerships.

3.1.3 Niche Relevance in Program Selection

When it comes to selecting affiliate programs, the relevance of the chosen niche plays a pivotal role in determining your success as an affiliate marketer. In this section, we delve into the importance of niche relevance in program selection and how alignment between your niche and the affiliate program enhances your chances of achieving affiliate marketing success.

Understanding Niche Relevance:

1. **Audience Alignment:** Your chosen niche represents a specific audience with particular interests, needs, and preferences. The affiliate programs you select should resonate with this audience to drive engagement and conversions.
2. **Content Synergy:** Niche relevance ensures synergy between your content and the products or services you're promoting. This alignment creates a seamless user experience and increases the likelihood of

conversions.

3. **Trust and Authority:** When your affiliate promotions align with your niche, you position yourself as a trusted authority within that niche. Visitors are more likely to trust recommendations that are closely related to your niche expertise.

The Benefits of Niche-Relevant Affiliate Programs:

1. **Higher Conversion Rates:** Affiliate programs that align with your niche are more likely to convert because they directly address your audience's needs and interests. Visitors are more inclined to take action when they perceive the product or service as relevant to their niche.

2. **Enhanced Credibility:** Promoting products or services that fit your niche enhances your credibility as an affiliate marketer. Your audience sees you as a knowledgeable source, increasing trust in your recommendations.

3. **Improved Content Engagement:** Niche-relevant programs provide you with the opportunity to create highly targeted and engaging content. This content speaks directly to your audience's pain points and aspirations, driving higher engagement levels.

4. **Long-Term Success:** Building a reputation within your niche takes time, and promoting niche-relevant products or services fosters long-term success. It ensures that your affiliate marketing efforts remain sustainable and continue to generate income over time.

Strategies for Ensuring Niche Relevance:

1. **Evaluate Affiliate Programs:** Before joining an affiliate program, assess the products or services it offers. Are they directly related to your niche? Do they solve

problems or fulfill needs within your niche?

2. **Match User Intent:** Consider the user's intent when they engage with your niche-related content. Ensure that the affiliate program's offerings align with the user's intent, whether it's seeking information, solving a problem, or making a purchase.

3. **Content Alignment:** Your content should seamlessly integrate affiliate promotions. Ensure that the affiliate product or service fits naturally within your content and addresses specific niche-related challenges.

4. **Test and Refine:** Continuously test the relevance and performance of affiliate programs within your niche. If certain programs aren't resonating with your audience, consider alternative options.

5. **Seek Niche-Specific Programs:** Explore affiliate networks or individual company websites that offer niche-specific programs. These programs are more likely to align with your niche and audience.

6. **Ask for Feedback:** Encourage audience feedback regarding the relevance and usefulness of your affiliate promotions. Use this feedback to fine-tune your program selections.

7. **Stay Informed:** Stay updated on industry trends and changes within your niche. New products or services may emerge that are highly relevant to your audience.

In conclusion, niche relevance is a cornerstone of successful affiliate marketing. By selecting affiliate programs that align with your chosen niche, you create a harmonious connection between your content and affiliate promotions. This alignment results in higher conversion rates, increased credibility, and long-term success as an affiliate marketer. Continuously assess and refine your program selections to ensure they resonate with your niche and meet your audience's needs effectively.

3.2 Selecting Prime Affiliate Partnerships

Choosing the right affiliate partnerships is a critical aspect of affiliate marketing success. In this section, we delve into the art of selecting prime affiliate partnerships that align with your niche, goals, and audience. Here, you will gain insights into the criteria and strategies for identifying and partnering with affiliate programs that offer the greatest potential for profitability and engagement.

3.2.1 Evaluating Program Credibility

In the world of affiliate marketing, trust and credibility are invaluable assets. The reputation of the affiliate programs you choose to partner with directly impacts your own reputation as an affiliate marketer. In this section, we delve into the vital importance of trust and credibility in affiliate programs and equip you with essential criteria and checks to assess the legitimacy of potential affiliate partnerships.

The Vital Role of Trust and Credibility:

1. **Audience Trust:** Your audience relies on your recommendations. When you promote products or services from trustworthy affiliate programs, your audience is more likely to trust your suggestions, leading to higher conversion rates.
2. **Reputation Management:** Your affiliate marketing efforts are an extension of your personal or brand reputation. Associating with credible programs enhances your reputation as a reliable source of information and solutions.
3. **Long-Term Success:** Credibility fosters long-term success. Building a sustainable affiliate marketing business requires maintaining a positive image and fostering trust with your audience over time.

Criteria for Assessing Program Credibility:

1. **Company Reputation:** Begin by researching the

reputation of the company or brand associated with the affiliate program. Look for online reviews, ratings, and customer feedback. A well-regarded company reflects positively on the program.

2. **Product or Service Quality:** Assess the quality and value of the products or services offered by the affiliate program. Are these offerings reputable, reliable, and genuinely beneficial to your audience? High-quality offerings enhance your credibility.

3. **Transparent Terms and Policies:** Scrutinize the program's terms and policies, including the commission structure, payment terms, and cookie duration. Transparency is a positive indicator of credibility and builds trust with affiliates.

4. **Clear Affiliate Guidelines:** Ensure the program provides clear and concise affiliate guidelines that outline the rules and expectations for affiliates. Transparency in expectations helps you understand your role and responsibilities.

5. **Support and Communication:** Evaluate the level of support and communication provided by the affiliate program. Reliable programs offer responsive customer support and maintain open communication channels with affiliates.

6. **Track Record:** Investigate the program's track record, specifically its history of payments to affiliates. Look for testimonials or case studies from other affiliates who have experienced success with the program.

7. **Payment Reliability:** Research the program's payment reliability. Examine whether they have a consistent history of making on-time and accurate payments to their affiliates.

8. **Affiliate Manager Availability:** If possible, reach out to the program's affiliate manager or designated contact person. A responsive and helpful affiliate manager indicates a program's commitment to its affiliates'

success.

9. **Community Feedback:** Explore online forums, social media groups, and communities where affiliate marketers share their experiences. Gather insights and feedback regarding the program's reputation and performance from your peers.

Checks to Assess Program Legitimacy:

1. **Domain Age and Website Security:** Check the age of the program's website domain. Older domains tend to be more reliable. Additionally, ensure that the program's website employs secure HTTPS.

2. **Contact Information:** Verify the presence of legitimate contact information on the program's website, including a physical address and contact email or phone number.

3. **Business Registration:** Confirm whether the company associated with the program is legally registered. This information is often available in the program's terms and conditions.

4. **Scam Alerts and Complaints:** Conduct thorough online research to search for any scam alerts or complaints related to the affiliate program. Investigate any red flags or concerns that arise during your search.

5. **Affiliate Agreement Review:** Carefully read and review the program's affiliate agreement. Ensure there are no clauses that seem unfair or raise concerns regarding your rights and obligations as an affiliate.

6. **Payment Proof:** Request payment proof from the program or inquire about their payment process to gauge reliability and authenticity.

In conclusion, evaluating the credibility of affiliate programs is a critical and non-negotiable aspect of affiliate marketing. By partnering with reputable and trustworthy programs, you safeguard your reputation and increase your potential for successful affiliate marketing endeavors. Employing the aforementioned criteria and conducting due diligence empowers you to confidently select affiliate partnerships that align with your niche and contribute to your long-term success as an affiliate marketer.

3.2.2 Product or Service Alignment

One of the fundamental principles of successful affiliate marketing is aligning the products or services you promote with your chosen niche. In this section, we underscore the necessity of this alignment and provide you with effective strategies to ensure the compatibility of affiliate offerings with your niche.

The Crucial Role of Product or Service Alignment:

1. **Audience Relevance:** Your chosen niche represents a specific audience with distinct interests, needs, and preferences. Affiliate offerings must resonate with this audience to be effective.
2. **Content Synergy:** When your affiliate promotions align with your niche, you create content that seamlessly integrates these promotions. This synergy enhances user experience and drives higher engagement and conversions.
3. **Credibility and Trust:** Promoting products or services that fit naturally within your niche enhances your credibility and trustworthiness. Your audience is more likely to trust recommendations that are directly relevant to your niche expertise.

Strategies for Ensuring Product or Service Compatibility:

1. **Thorough Evaluation and Audience Alignment:** Before promoting any product or service, evaluate its features and relevance to your niche while ensuring it addresses the needs of your audience effectively.

2. **Personal Use and Contextual Promotion:** Whenever possible, use the product or service yourself for authentic recommendations. Ensure that your affiliate promotions seamlessly fit within your content by aligning product themes with your content topics.

3. **Audience Intent and Feedback:** Understand your audience's intent when engaging with your niche content and seek feedback to fine-tune your affiliate selections based on audience preferences.

4. **Tailored Offerings and Timely Promotions:** Match affiliate offerings to specific audience segments within your niche and synchronize promotions with niche trends or events for relevance.

5. **Consistent Branding and Regular Updates:** Maintain consistent branding across your niche content and promotions, and regularly review and update your affiliate offerings to ensure ongoing relevance within your niche.

In summary, product or service alignment is an indispensable aspect of affiliate marketing success. By ensuring that the products or services you promote seamlessly integrate with your niche, you create a cohesive and trustworthy affiliate marketing strategy. Implement these strategies to guarantee that your affiliate offerings align with your audience's interests and needs, ultimately contributing to higher engagement and conversions in your affiliate marketing efforts.

3.2.3 Commission Structures and Payment Methods

Understanding commission structures and payment methods is essential when selecting affiliate programs. In this section, we'll explain different commission structures, such as CPA (Cost Per Action), CPS (Cost Per Sale), and CPL (Cost Per Lead), and discuss the significance of payment methods and frequency in affiliate marketing.

Different Commission Structures:

1. **CPA (Cost Per Action):** CPA is a commission structure where affiliates earn a fee for specific actions taken by referred customers. These actions can include making a purchase, filling out a form, subscribing, or downloading an app. CPA offers are attractive as they reward affiliates for tangible results.
2. **CPS (Cost Per Sale):** CPS is the most common commission structure in affiliate marketing. Affiliates receive a percentage of the sales generated through their referral links. This structure is straightforward and aligns with e-commerce and product-focused niches.
3. **CPL (Cost Per Lead):** CPL is based on lead generation. Affiliates are compensated when they refer potential customers who take a specific action, such as signing up for a newsletter, filling out a survey, or requesting more information. CPL is often used in industries like insurance or finance.
4. **CPC (Cost Per Click):** While less common, some affiliate programs pay on a per-click basis. Affiliates earn a fee for every click on their referral links, regardless of whether it leads to a sale. CPC can be suitable for niches where direct sales aren't the primary goal.

Importance of Payment Methods and Frequency:

1. **Payment Methods:** Affiliates should consider the payment methods offered by affiliate programs. Common payment methods include PayPal, direct bank transfers, checks, and digital wallets. Ensure that the chosen method is convenient and accessible for you, considering any associated fees.
2. **Payment Frequency:** Payment frequency refers to

how often you receive your earnings from the affiliate program. Payment schedules vary, with some programs offering monthly, bi-weekly, weekly, or even daily payouts. Consider your financial needs and preferences when selecting a program with the appropriate payment frequency.

3. **Minimum Payment Threshold:** Many affiliate programs set a minimum payment threshold. This is the minimum amount you must earn before you can receive a payout. Be aware of this threshold and choose programs that align with your earning goals.

4. **Currency and Conversion:** If you have an international audience, check whether the affiliate program supports multiple currencies and offers currency conversion options. This ensures that you receive payments in your preferred currency.

5. **Hold Periods:** Some affiliate programs have hold periods during which they verify the validity of referred sales or leads. Understand these hold periods and factor them into your cash flow planning.

6. **Performance Metrics:** Consider the program's performance metrics when evaluating payment. Some programs may offer tiered commissions based on performance milestones, such as reaching a specific number of referrals or achieving higher conversion rates.

7. **Recurring Commissions:** In certain niches, recurring commissions can be highly lucrative. These commissions provide affiliates with ongoing income for subscription-based products or services. Assess whether the program offers such opportunities.

8. **Referral Lifetime Value:** Determine if the program has a referral lifetime value policy. This means you continue to earn commissions from referred customers on future purchases, providing a source of passive income.

9. **Payment Transparency:** Choose programs that offer transparent reporting and payment tracking. This ensures that you can monitor your earnings, conversions, and pending payments effectively.

In conclusion, commission structures and payment methods are integral aspects of affiliate program selection. Consider the commission structure that best aligns with your niche and audience, and evaluate payment methods and frequency to ensure they suit your financial needs and preferences. A well-structured payment system not only rewards your affiliate efforts but also contributes to a smooth and profitable affiliate marketing experience.

3.2.4 Affiliate Program Terms and Conditions

Reading and understanding an affiliate program's terms and conditions is a critical aspect of affiliate marketing. In this section, we emphasize the significance of thoroughly reviewing program terms and provide guidance on interpreting affiliate agreements and policies.

The Significance of Reading and Understanding Program Terms:

1. **Legal Obligations:** Affiliate agreements are legally binding contracts between you and the affiliate program. By agreeing to the terms, you commit to following specific guidelines and policies. Failing to adhere to these obligations can result in consequences, including the termination of your partnership.
2. **Compliance and Ethical Practices:** Program terms outline ethical and compliance standards. Understanding these standards is essential to ensure that your affiliate marketing practices align with industry regulations and best practices.
3. **Payment Terms:** The terms and conditions specify payment details, including commission

rates, payment frequency, and minimum payout thresholds. Knowing these details helps you manage your financial expectations and plan your affiliate marketing strategy effectively.

4. **Cookie and Tracking Policies:** Many affiliate programs use cookies to track referrals and attribute commissions. Understanding the program's cookie duration and tracking mechanisms ensures you can monitor the performance of your referrals accurately.

5. **Content and Promotion Guidelines:** Affiliate programs often have guidelines regarding how you can promote their products or services. These guidelines may include restrictions on certain promotional methods or content types. Adhering to these guidelines prevents potential conflicts and violations.

6. **Termination and Dispute Resolution:** The terms outline the circumstances under which the program can terminate your affiliate partnership. Understanding these conditions helps you mitigate risks and resolve disputes should they arise.

Guidance on Interpreting Affiliate Agreements and Policies:

1. **Read and Understand Thoroughly:**

Begin by carefully reading the entire affiliate agreement and associated policies. Pay attention to even the smallest details, as they can have significant implications for your partnership. Understanding the agreement is fundamental to a successful affiliate marketing venture.

2. **Focus on Key Terms and Obligations:**

Identify key terms or phrases used in the agreement and create clear definitions for them. Take note of your obligations as an affiliate, encompassing content creation, promotional methods, and adherence to program policies. Ensuring a precise understanding of these elements is vital.

3. **Commission, Payment, and Promotion Details:**

Examine the commission structure, payment terms, and promotion guidelines outlined in the agreement. Understand commission rates, payment methods, frequencies, and any hold periods for earnings. Align your marketing practices with program guidelines to prevent issues.

4. **Termination Clauses and Dispute Resolution:**

Review termination clauses and conditions to comprehend the circumstances under which your partnership can be terminated. Be aware of dispute resolution mechanisms, such as mediation or arbitration processes, and how to address issues if they arise. Document the agreement and maintain records for reference.

5. **Seek Clarification When Needed:**

Don't hesitate to reach out to the program's affiliate manager or support team if you have uncertainties or require clarification on specific terms. They can provide valuable insights and guidance. Additionally, stay informed about any updates or changes to the program's terms and conditions to ensure ongoing compliance.

In conclusion, reading and understanding affiliate program terms and conditions is an essential responsibility of affiliate marketers. These agreements govern your partnership and influence your affiliate marketing practices. By thoroughly reviewing and interpreting program terms, you can navigate your affiliate marketing journey with confidence, maintain compliance, and build a successful and ethical affiliate marketing business.

3.3 Negotiating Your Commission

In the world of affiliate marketing, negotiation plays a pivotal role in shaping your earnings and forging mutually beneficial partnerships. In this section, we explore the art of negotiating your commission within affiliate programs. Discover effective strategies and tactics to maximize your affiliate earnings and advocate for fair compensation for your valuable marketing efforts.

3.3.1 The Art of Negotiation

Negotiation is a skill that holds tremendous potential within the realm of affiliate marketing. In this section, we introduce the concept of negotiation in affiliate marketing and delve into the compelling benefits of negotiating for higher commissions.

Introduction to Negotiation in Affiliate Marketing:

Affiliate marketing is a dynamic and evolving field where both affiliates and affiliate programs seek to maximize their returns. Negotiation serves as a strategic tool in this landscape, allowing affiliates to advocate for terms that reflect the value they bring to the partnership. The negotiation process involves discussions between affiliates and program managers to arrive at mutually agreeable commission rates, terms, and conditions.

The Potential Benefits of Negotiating Higher Commissions:

1. **Increased Earnings:** Negotiating for higher commissions directly impacts your earnings. By securing a more favorable commission structure, you stand to earn more for each referred sale, lead, or action.
2. **Enhanced Motivation:** Knowing that you're compensated fairly for your efforts can boost your motivation and dedication to your affiliate marketing endeavors. This increased motivation often translates into better performance and more successful campaigns.
3. **Competitive Edge:** Negotiating higher commissions can give you a competitive edge in your niche. With the potential to offer better incentives to your audience, you can outperform competitors and capture a larger share of the market.

4. **Resource Allocation:** Higher commissions enable you to allocate more resources, such as time and budget, to your affiliate marketing initiatives. This can lead to improved content quality, expanded promotional efforts, and greater reach.

5. **Loyalty and Longevity:** Affiliate programs that are willing to negotiate and accommodate affiliates' requests often foster loyalty and long-term partnerships. Establishing a reputation as a valued affiliate can lead to ongoing collaborations and sustained income.

6. **Risk Mitigation:** Negotiating commissions can serve as a buffer against economic fluctuations or changes in the program's terms. It provides a degree of financial security, especially if you have established a steady stream of referrals.

7. **Strategic Positioning:** Negotiating higher commissions is a strategic move that positions you as a knowledgeable and assertive affiliate marketer. This can positively impact how program managers perceive your value within their network.

8. **Alignment with Effort:** Negotiating higher commissions aligns your compensation with the effort and resources you invest in promoting affiliate products or services. It ensures that your earnings reflect your marketing expertise.

Effective Strategies for Negotiation:

1. **Know Your Worth:** Conduct thorough research to assess the value you bring to the affiliate program. Consider your conversion rates, audience engagement, and the quality of your content.

2. **Build Relationships:** Cultivate strong relationships with program managers or affiliate contacts. Effective communication and rapport can facilitate

negotiations.

3. **Highlight Past Success:** Showcase your past successes and the positive impact you've had on the program's performance. Provide concrete data and case studies if available.

4. **Propose Value-Based Arguments:** Base your negotiation on the value you generate for the program. Explain how higher commissions would result in increased revenue for both parties.

5. **Be Professional and Respectful:** Approach negotiations with professionalism and respect. Avoid confrontational or aggressive tactics, as they can harm your reputation.

6. **Consider Win-Win Scenarios:** Strive for mutually beneficial outcomes. Look for solutions that benefit both you and the program, such as performance-based incentives.

7. **Be Prepared to Compromise:** While aiming for higher commissions, be open to compromise. Flexibility can lead to productive negotiations and fruitful partnerships.

In conclusion, negotiation is a valuable skill in affiliate marketing, offering the potential for increased earnings, motivation, and competitiveness. By effectively negotiating for higher commissions, you can align your compensation with your affiliate marketing efforts and secure partnerships that are both rewarding and sustainable.

3.3.2 Demonstrating Value to Merchants

Effectively demonstrating your value to affiliate program managers is a key aspect of successful negotiation in affiliate marketing. In this section, we explore strategies for affiliates to showcase their worth and highlight their potential to drive increased sales for affiliate programs.

Explaining Your Value to Affiliate Program Managers:

1. **Conversion Rates:** Begin by sharing your conversion rates and the number of leads or sales you've generated for the program. High conversion rates indicate your effectiveness in turning referrals into customers.
2. **Audience Engagement:** Emphasize your ability to engage and nurture your audience. Explain how your content and promotional efforts resonate with your niche and create a sense of trust and authority.
3. **Content Quality:** Highlight the quality of your content, whether it's blog posts, videos, reviews, or social media posts. Well-crafted content not only attracts but also converts visitors into customers.
4. **Targeted Audience:** Describe your audience's alignment with the program's products or services. A targeted and relevant audience is more likely to result in successful conversions.
5. **Consistency:** Showcase your consistency in promoting the program's offerings. Regular and reliable promotional efforts demonstrate your commitment and reliability as an affiliate.
6. **Unique Marketing Channels:** If you use unique or innovative marketing channels, share them with program managers. Differentiation in your promotional methods can set you apart.
7. **Case Studies and Success Stories:** Provide case studies or success stories that illustrate the impact of your affiliate marketing efforts. Real-world examples can be persuasive.

Strategies for Showcasing Increased Sales Potential:

1. **Data-Driven Performance:** Leverage data to support your claims and demonstrate your ability to drive increased sales. Present analytics and performance

metrics showcasing growth trends and improvements over time. A data-backed approach provides credibility and confidence in your sales potential.

2. **Market Research for Growth:** Conduct thorough market research to identify growth opportunities within your niche. Share your findings with program managers to illustrate your proactive approach to expanding sales. Market insights are essential in aligning your efforts with the program's goals.

3. **Seasonal and Trend Alignment:** Propose seasonal or trend-specific campaigns that can boost sales during peak periods and align with the program's products or services. Showcase how these campaigns can capitalize on market trends and consumer behavior. Seasonal strategies highlight your adaptability and potential for sales growth.

4. **Innovative Marketing Tactics:** Introduce innovative marketing strategies aligned with the program's objectives that have the potential to increase sales. Explain how these tactics can set you apart and drive customer engagement. Innovation in marketing showcases your commitment to driving results.

5. **Focus on Loyalty and Expansion:** Highlight your capability not only to drive initial sales but also to nurture customer loyalty and retention. Describe strategies for turning first-time buyers into repeat customers, emphasizing long-term growth. Loyalty-building measures demonstrate sustainable sales potential.

6. **Transparent Communication:** Maintain open and transparent communication with program managers. Solicit feedback and collaborate on improvements to your promotional efforts. Effective communication ensures alignment with the program's goals and foster.

By effectively communicating your value and demonstrating

your potential to increase sales, you strengthen your position during negotiations. Affiliate program managers are more likely to consider higher commissions when they see evidence of your impact and your commitment to mutual success.

3.3.3 Negotiation Best Practices

Negotiating commission rates in affiliate marketing requires finesse and professionalism. In this section, we share negotiation best practices, emphasizing effective communication and providing tips for conducting negotiations professionally and successfully.

Effective Communication in Negotiation:

1. **Prepare Thoroughly:** Before entering negotiations, gather all necessary information, including your performance metrics, audience demographics, and industry benchmarks. Being well-prepared instills confidence and competence.
2. **Clear and Concise Communication:** Express your points clearly and concisely. Avoid ambiguity or vagueness. Ensure that your requests and proposals are easily understood.
3. **Active Listening:** Effective negotiation involves active listening. Pay close attention to the program manager's responses and concerns. Address their points thoughtfully.
4. **Empathy:** Understand the program manager's perspective and objectives. Show empathy and flexibility to find mutually beneficial solutions.
5. **Respectful Tone:** Maintain a respectful and professional tone throughout the negotiation. Avoid confrontational or aggressive language.

Tips for Negotiating Commission Rates:

1. **Data-Backed Request:** Begin with a strong

understanding of your performance metrics, conversion rates, and the revenue you bring to the program. Support your negotiation with data, demonstrating your value to the program.

2. **Start Reasonably:** Initiate negotiations with a fair and justifiable request, avoiding overly aggressive demands. A moderate increase in commission rates is often a more effective starting point.

3. **Showcase Achievements:** Highlight your past successes and contributions to the program's growth. Provide specific examples and data to illustrate your impact, strengthening your case for higher rates.

4. **Mutual Benefits:** Explain how an increase in commission rates benefits both you and the program by incentivizing greater promotion of their products or services. Emphasize the value of a win-win scenario.

5. **Performance-Based Tiers:** Suggest tiered commission structures tied to performance milestones, aligning your compensation with results. This approach provides motivation for continued growth.

6. **Timing Considerations:** If base rate increases are challenging, propose temporary boosts during special promotions or peak seasons. This flexible approach can be more acceptable to program managers.

7. **Patience in Negotiation:** Be patient during negotiations, allowing room for constructive discussions and avoiding hasty decisions. Effective negotiation often requires time for both parties to reach a consensus.

8. **Explore Alternatives:** If higher commission rates aren't feasible, explore alternative forms of compensation, such as bonuses or performance-based rewards. Flexibility can lead to mutually beneficial agreements.

9. **Formalize Agreements:** Once a negotiation concludes, formalize the agreed-upon terms in writing through

a clear and detailed contract or addendum. This provides clarity and accountability for both parties.

Remember that successful negotiation in affiliate marketing is not just about securing higher commissions but also about building and nurturing long-lasting partnerships. Approaching negotiations professionally and ethically benefits both you and the affiliate program, fostering an environment of mutual trust and collaboration.

3.3.4 Monitoring and Adjusting Commissions

Monitoring commission performance and being prepared to make adjustments is a crucial aspect of maintaining a successful affiliate partnership. In this section, we delve into the significance of monitoring commissions and provide guidance on when and how to request commission adjustments based on results.

The Importance of Monitoring Commission Performance:

1. **Performance Evaluation:** Regularly monitoring commission performance allows affiliates to assess the effectiveness of their promotional efforts. It provides insights into which strategies are working and which may need refinement.
2. **Tracking ROI:** By analyzing commissions in relation to marketing expenses, affiliates can calculate their return on investment (ROI). This helps in determining the profitability of their campaigns.
3. **Identifying Trends:** Monitoring commission data over time helps affiliates identify trends, such as seasonal variations or changes in consumer behavior. This information can inform campaign planning.
4. **Optimization Opportunities:** Understanding commission performance enables affiliates to optimize their strategies. They can allocate resources to the most successful campaigns and make data-driven

adjustments.

When to Request Commission Adjustments:

1. **Exceeding Targets:** If you consistently exceed the targets set by the affiliate program and your performance significantly contributes to their success, it's appropriate to consider requesting a commission increase.

2. **Consistent Growth:** If your affiliate marketing efforts consistently drive growth in sales or leads for the program, it indicates your value. In such cases, commission adjustments can be warranted.

3. **Market Changes:** If external factors, such as changes in the market landscape or increased competition, affect your ability to generate sales, consider negotiating for a higher commission to offset the challenges.

4. **Expanding Reach:** When you expand your reach, audience, or marketing channels, and this expansion leads to increased conversions, it's an opportune time to discuss commission adjustments.

5. **New Campaigns:** If you introduce innovative campaigns or strategies that result in substantial sales growth, present the data as evidence when requesting commission adjustments.

How to Request Commission Adjustments:

1. **Prepare Data:** Gather data that supports your request, including performance metrics, conversion rates, and revenue generated for the program. Use clear, concise, and persuasive arguments.

2. **Schedule a Meeting:** Reach out to the program manager or contact person to schedule a meeting or discussion. Express your intent to discuss commission adjustments professionally.

3. **Present Your Case:** During the meeting, present your

case for commission adjustments. Explain the reasons, provide data, and highlight your commitment to the program's success.

4. **Propose a Solution:** Suggest a commission adjustment that aligns with your performance and expectations. Be prepared to negotiate and find a mutually agreeable solution.

5. **Emphasize Mutual Benefit:** Highlight how the proposed commission adjustment benefits both you and the program. Stress the potential for increased sales and revenue.

6. **Formalize in Writing:** Once an agreement is reached, formalize the commission adjustments in writing. Create a clear and detailed contract or addendum outlining the revised terms.

7. **Maintain Transparency:** Continue to maintain open and transparent communication with the program manager. Provide updates on your performance and adherence to the agreed-upon terms.

8. **Evaluate Results:** After the adjustments, closely monitor the impact on your earnings and the program's performance. Assess whether the changes align with your expectations and ROI goals.

9. **Revisit as Needed:** If your performance continues to exceed expectations, or if market conditions change, revisit the negotiation process as necessary to ensure fair compensation.

Remember that commission adjustments should be approached professionally and with a focus on mutual benefit. A transparent and data-driven approach enhances the chances of a successful outcome. Additionally, maintaining a positive and cooperative relationship with the program manager is essential for ongoing success in affiliate marketing.

CHAPTER 4: CRAFTING COMPELLING CONTENT

In the ever-evolving landscape of affiliate marketing, crafting compelling content remains an essential skill for driving conversions and engaging audiences. In this chapter, we will explore the pivotal role of content in affiliate marketing and provide invaluable insights into creating content that captivates and converts. From understanding content's significance to mastering the art of promotion, this chapter is your guide to elevating your affiliate marketing strategy through impactful content creation.

4.1 Content's Crucial Role

The role of content in affiliate marketing cannot be overstated —it serves as the bridge between affiliates, products, and consumers. In this section, we delve into the pivotal role that content plays within the affiliate marketing ecosystem. We'll explore how well-crafted content serves as the linchpin for attracting, informing, and ultimately persuading your audience to take action.

4.1.1 The Content Connection

Content is the beating heart of affiliate marketing, serving as the essential connection between affiliates, products or services, and the target audience. In this section, we'll explore the pivotal role of content in affiliate marketing, highlighting how quality content establishes trust, fosters engagement, and drives conversions.

The Pivotal Role of Content in Affiliate Marketing:

1. **Information Dissemination:** Content acts as the primary vehicle for conveying information about the products or services you're promoting as an affiliate. It educates your audience about the benefits, features, and value of what you're recommending.
2. **Audience Engagement:** Engaging content captures the attention of your audience and encourages them to interact with your affiliate offerings. It serves as a catalyst for building relationships and loyalty.
3. **Trust Building:** High-quality content establishes trust and credibility with your audience. When you provide valuable and accurate information, you position yourself as a reliable source of recommendations.
4. **Audience Segmentation:** Content allows you to segment your audience effectively. You can tailor content to different demographics, interests, and needs, ensuring that your affiliate promotions resonate with specific groups.
5. **Problem Solving:** Content can address the pain points and problems your audience faces, demonstrating how the promoted product or service offers solutions. This problem-solving approach is compelling to potential customers.
6. **SEO and Visibility:** Well-optimized content can improve your website's search engine rankings, making it easier for your target audience to find your affiliate recommendations when searching online.
7. **Authority Establishment:** Consistent and authoritative content in your niche establishes you as an expert in your field. This authority bolsters your

influence and persuasiveness as an affiliate marketer.

How Quality Content Establishes Trust and Engagement:

1. **Informative and Valuable:** Quality content provides genuine value to your audience. It offers insights, information, or entertainment that resonates with their interests and needs.
2. **Accuracy and Transparency:** Trustworthy content is accurate and transparent. It presents information truthfully and openly, without misleading or exaggerating claims.
3. **Relevance:** Relevant content addresses the specific interests and concerns of your target audience. It speaks directly to their needs, making them more likely to engage and take action.
4. **Engagement Elements:** Incorporating elements like compelling storytelling, visuals, videos, and interactive features keeps your audience engaged. Engaging content encourages longer visit durations and return visits.
5. **Credible Sources:** Backing up your content with credible sources, data, or expert opinions reinforces trust. It demonstrates that your recommendations are well-researched and grounded in reputable information.
6. **Consistency:** Consistency in content quality and messaging builds trust over time. Regularly delivering valuable content establishes a reliable expectation with your audience.
7. **Call to Action (CTA):** Effective content includes clear and persuasive calls to action. A well-placed CTA guides your audience toward taking the desired steps, such as clicking an affiliate link or making a purchase.
8. **Feedback and Interaction:** Encourage feedback, comments, and interaction with your content.

> Respond to audience inquiries and engage in conversations to foster a sense of community and trust.

9. **Personalization:** Tailor content to your audience's preferences and needs. Personalized content enhances engagement and connection.

In conclusion, content is the linchpin of affiliate marketing, serving as the conduit for information, engagement, and trust. By consistently delivering high-quality, trustworthy content that resonates with your target audience, you can establish yourself as a credible affiliate marketer and effectively drive conversions. Content creation is an art, and mastering it is essential for success in the affiliate marketing landscape.

4.1.2 Content Marketing vs. Traditional Advertising

In the realm of affiliate marketing, the approach to promoting products or services has evolved significantly, shifting from traditional advertising methods to content marketing. In this section, we'll contrast content marketing with traditional advertising, shedding light on the distinct approaches and emphasizing the benefits of providing value through content.

Contrasting Content Marketing with Traditional Advertising:

1. Approach to Promotion:

- **Content Marketing:** Content marketing is an approach that focuses on creating valuable and informative content that resonates with the target audience. It aims to educate, entertain, or solve problems, indirectly leading the audience towards making informed purchasing decisions. Content marketing is about building trust and nurturing long-term relationships.
- **Traditional Advertising:** Traditional advertising relies on more direct and promotional tactics. It often

involves paid advertisements, such as TV commercials, billboards, radio spots, and print media. These advertisements aim to capture attention and drive immediate sales through persuasive messaging.

2. Engagement and Interactivity:

- **Content Marketing:** Content marketing encourages audience engagement and interactivity. It invites readers to explore, learn, and interact with the content through comments, sharing, and discussions. It fosters a sense of community and involvement.
- **Traditional Advertising:** Traditional advertising typically offers limited opportunities for engagement. It's a one-way communication method where the audience receives the message without active participation.

3. Value-Oriented Approach:

- **Content Marketing:** Content marketing places a strong emphasis on providing value to the audience. It seeks to inform, entertain, or address specific needs and questions. The value provided builds trust and positions the affiliate marketer as a valuable resource.
- **Traditional Advertising:** Traditional advertising often prioritizes self-promotion and the features or benefits of the product or service. While it can be persuasive, it may not always provide substantial value beyond the promotional message.

4. Longevity and Sustainability:

- **Content Marketing:** Quality content created as part of content marketing can have a longer shelf life. It continues to provide value and attract organic traffic over time. Evergreen content, in particular, remains relevant for extended periods.

- **Traditional Advertising:** Traditional advertising tends to have a shorter lifespan. Once the ad campaign ends, its impact diminishes, and it requires ongoing investment for sustained results.

Benefits of Providing Value Through Content:

1. **Establishing Trust:** Content marketing builds trust by offering valuable, non-promotional information. Trust is a cornerstone of successful affiliate marketing.
2. **Audience Engagement:** Content encourages interaction, feedback, and discussions, fostering a sense of community and engagement.
3. **Educational Value:** Content can educate the audience, addressing their questions and concerns. Informed consumers are more likely to make confident purchase decisions.
4. **Sustainable Impact:** Quality content can continue to attract and inform your audience over time, extending the reach of your affiliate promotions.
5. **Positioning as an Authority:** Consistently providing value through content establishes you as an authority in your niche, which can lead to increased influence and conversions.
6. **Improved SEO:** Valuable content that answers specific queries can improve your website's search engine rankings, driving organic traffic and potential conversions.

In conclusion, content marketing and traditional advertising represent distinct approaches within the affiliate marketing landscape. While traditional advertising can be effective, content marketing's emphasis on providing value, building trust, and fostering engagement aligns well with the evolving expectations of today's digital consumers. Affiliates who prioritize value-driven content are better positioned to succeed in building long-lasting, profitable relationships with their audience.

4.1.3 Building Authority through Content

Quality content has the remarkable power to position affiliate marketers as authorities within their niches. In this section, we'll emphasize how creating valuable content can establish affiliates as trusted experts and provide examples of successful affiliates who have leveraged content to attain authority status.

Emphasizing the Authority-Building Potential of Quality Content:

1. **In-Depth Knowledge Sharing:** By consistently producing content that offers deep insights, addresses specific questions, and provides comprehensive information, affiliates demonstrate their expertise and in-depth knowledge of their niches.
2. **Problem Solving:** Quality content often focuses on solving common problems or challenges within a niche. When affiliates provide effective solutions through their content, they become a go-to resource for their audience.
3. **Credibility:** Affiliates who create well-researched and accurate content earn credibility. This credibility is further enhanced when content is supported by reputable sources, data, or expert opinions.
4. **Consistency:** The ongoing creation of valuable content establishes a pattern of consistency, showing that affiliates are committed to serving their audience's needs. Consistency is a hallmark of authority.
5. **Audience Engagement:** Engaging with the audience through comments, discussions, and feedback demonstrates a commitment to helping and connecting with the community. This engagement builds trust and strengthens authority.

Examples of Successful Affiliates Leveraging Content for

Authority:

1. **Neil Patel:** Neil Patel is renowned for his expertise in digital marketing. Through his blog, podcasts, and videos, he consistently provides actionable advice and insights on various aspects of online marketing, earning him a reputation as an authority in the field.

2. **Pat Flynn (Smart Passive Income):** Pat Flynn's blog and podcast, Smart Passive Income, are dedicated to helping individuals achieve financial independence through online businesses. His transparent sharing of income reports and detailed case studies has solidified his position as a trusted authority in online entrepreneurship.

3. **Brian Dean (Backlinko):** Brian Dean's blog, Backlinko, is a treasure trove of SEO knowledge. He's known for his in-depth guides and case studies, which have earned him recognition as an authority in the world of search engine optimization.

4. **Rand Fishkin (Moz):** Rand Fishkin, the co-founder of Moz, is a thought leader in the field of SEO. His contributions through Moz's blog, Whiteboard Friday videos, and industry presentations have established him as a prominent authority on SEO and inbound marketing.

5. **Ahrefs (Blog and YouTube Channel):** Ahrefs, a leading SEO software company, has created a wealth of educational content on their blog and YouTube channel. Their data-driven approach and in-depth tutorials have positioned them as authoritative voices in the SEO community.

6. **Healthline (Health and Wellness Niche):** Healthline, a popular health and wellness affiliate, offers a wealth of authoritative content. Their articles are medically reviewed, and they've built trust with their audience by providing reliable health information and resources.

These examples illustrate how affiliates from diverse niches have leveraged quality content to establish authority. They have earned the trust and respect of their audiences by consistently delivering valuable, accurate, and engaging content. By following in their footsteps, affiliate marketers can similarly build their authority and enhance their affiliate marketing success.

4.2 Crafting Captivating Content

In the world of affiliate marketing, crafting content that captivates and resonates with your target audience is a skill of paramount importance. This chapter delves into the art and science of crafting captivating content that not only grabs attention but also compels action. From storytelling techniques to effective headlines, this section provides essential insights to help you create content that truly engages and converts.

4.2.1 Content Types for Affiliate Marketing

In the realm of affiliate marketing, the versatility of content is a treasure trove waiting to be explored. To effectively engage your audience and drive conversions, it's essential to leverage various content types that align with your niche and resonate with your target audience. In this section, we'll introduce a spectrum of content types suitable for affiliate marketing, ranging from blog posts and videos to product reviews and more.

1. Blog Posts:
- **Introduction:** Blog posts are the cornerstone of content marketing for many affiliates. They allow you to create informative, engaging, and SEO-friendly content. Blogging is versatile, accommodating a wide range of topics and niches.
- **Usage:** Use blog posts to provide valuable information, answer questions, and share your insights. They are ideal for in-depth articles, how-to guides, and

educational content.

- **Examples:** Affiliate marketers often use blog posts to review products, compare alternatives, offer tutorials, and share industry news.

2. Videos:

- **Introduction:** Video content has seen explosive growth in recent years. It offers a dynamic way to connect with your audience and convey information effectively. Video platforms like YouTube are popular choices for affiliate marketing through video.
- **Usage:** Create videos to review products, demonstrate their use, offer tutorials, share personal experiences, or conduct interviews. Videos allow you to showcase products visually.
- **Examples:** You can create unboxing videos, product demonstrations, comparison videos, and informative vlogs.

3. Product Reviews:

- **Introduction:** Product reviews are a staple in affiliate marketing. They provide detailed insights into the pros and cons of products or services, helping your audience make informed decisions.
- **Usage:** Write comprehensive product reviews that highlight features, benefits, and real-world experiences. Be transparent and honest in your evaluations.
- **Examples:** You can review a wide range of products, from tech gadgets and fashion items to digital services and software.

4. Tutorials and How-To Guides:

- **Introduction:** Tutorials and how-to guides are valuable for demonstrating the practical use of products or services. They establish you as an authority and offer step-by-step instructions.

- **Usage:** Create tutorials that show your audience how to solve specific problems or achieve desired outcomes using the affiliate products or services you promote.
- **Examples:** Examples include software tutorials, DIY guides, and cooking recipes that incorporate affiliate products.

5. Infographics:

- **Introduction:** Infographics are visual representations of information. They are effective in presenting data, statistics, or complex concepts in a visually appealing and easily digestible format.
- **Usage:** Use infographics to convey key information, compare products, or showcase the benefits of a service. Infographics are highly shareable on social media.
- **Examples:** You can create infographics for product comparisons, industry statistics, or informative visual guides.

6. Email Newsletters:

- **Introduction:** Email marketing remains a powerful tool for affiliate marketers. Email newsletters allow you to maintain a direct line of communication with your subscribers.
- **Usage:** Send newsletters that include affiliate promotions, product recommendations, and valuable content to engage and nurture your email list.
- **Examples:** Share curated lists of affiliate products, exclusive discounts, or personalized recommendations.

7. Social Media Content:

- **Introduction:** Social media platforms are fertile ground for affiliate marketing. Short-form content, images, and stories on platforms like Instagram, Facebook, and Twitter can drive traffic and

conversions.
- **Usage:** Share affiliate links, showcase products in action, and engage with your audience through posts, stories, and live videos.
- **Examples:** Create visually appealing posts that promote affiliate products, conduct giveaways, or host Q&A sessions.

8. Podcasts:
- **Introduction:** Podcasts are a rising star in content marketing. They offer a convenient way for your audience to consume content on the go.
- **Usage:** Host podcast episodes that discuss relevant topics, interview industry experts, or review products and services. Include affiliate links in podcast show notes.
- **Examples:** Podcasts can cover a wide array of niches, from technology and business to health and entertainment.

9. Webinars and Live Streams:
- **Introduction:** Webinars and live streams enable real-time interaction with your audience. They can be used to educate, entertain, and promote affiliate products.
- **Usage:** Host webinars that dive deep into niche-related subjects or showcase products through live demonstrations. Include affiliate links and exclusive offers for attendees.
- **Examples:** Webinars can focus on educational topics, industry trends, or specific product launches.

By incorporating a mix of these content types into your affiliate marketing strategy, you can cater to diverse audience preferences and provide valuable information in various formats. Experiment with different content types to discover what resonates best with your target audience and drives the highest conversion rates.

4.2.2 Content Creation Strategies

Creating compelling affiliate content requires a thoughtful approach that addresses the specific needs, interests, and pain points of your audience. In this section, we'll delve into content creation strategies that will help you brainstorm, plan, and execute content that resonates with your target audience, ultimately driving engagement and conversions.

1. **Audience-Centric Approach:**
   - **Understand Your Audience:** Begin by gaining a deep understanding of your target audience. Identify their demographics, preferences, and pain points. Use tools like surveys, social media insights, and analytics to gather valuable data.
   - **Create Buyer Personas:** Develop detailed buyer personas that represent different segments of your audience. These personas help you tailor your content to specific needs and preferences.
   - **Address Pain Points:** Identify the challenges, problems, and questions your audience faces within your niche. Your content should offer solutions, insights, and guidance to address these pain points.

2. **Keyword Research:**
   - **Keyword Planning:** Conduct thorough keyword research to identify the topics and search terms relevant to your niche. Tools like Google Keyword Planner, SEMrush, and Ahrefs can assist in this process.
   - **Long-Tail Keywords:** Focus on long-tail keywords that reflect specific queries and intent. These keywords often have lower competition and can attract highly targeted traffic.
   - **Content Optimization:** Integrate selected keywords naturally into your content, including titles,

headings, and body text. This optimization improves your content's search engine visibility.

3. Content Calendar:

- **Plan Ahead:** Create a content calendar that outlines your content strategy for weeks or months in advance. This planning ensures consistent content production.
- **Seasonal and Trend-Based Content:** Incorporate seasonal and trend-based topics into your calendar to remain relevant and capitalize on timely opportunities.
- **Diverse Content Mix:** Balance different types of content, such as blog posts, videos, and social media updates, within your calendar to cater to varied audience preferences.

4. Competitor Analysis:

- **Analyze Competitor Content:** Study your competitors' content to identify gaps and opportunities. Look for topics they have covered well and areas where you can provide a unique perspective or offer more comprehensive information.
- **Identify Successful Content:** Determine which content pieces have garnered the most engagement and shares among your competitors. Emulate successful content formats while adding your own unique twist.

5. Content Structure and Formatting:

- **Clear Structure:** Organize your content with a clear and logical structure. Use headings, subheadings, bullet points, and numbered lists to break down information and improve readability.
- **Visual Elements:** Incorporate visuals such as images, infographics, and videos to enhance your

content's appeal and convey information more effectively.

- **Mobile Optimization:** Ensure that your content is mobile-friendly. Many users access content on smartphones, and mobile optimization is crucial for a positive user experience.

6. Value-Driven Content:

- **Provide Value:** Always prioritize providing value to your audience. Address their questions, offer insights, and share your expertise to establish trust and authority.
- **Educational Content:** Consider creating educational content that teaches your audience new skills, solves problems, or explains complex concepts related to your niche.
- **Unique Perspectives:** Share your unique experiences, case studies, or personal insights to differentiate your content from competitors.

7. Engagement and Interaction:

- **Encourage Interaction:** Actively engage with your audience through comments, social media, and email. Respond to questions and feedback promptly to build a sense of community.
- **User-Generated Content:** Encourage users to share their experiences or contributions related to your niche. Highlight user-generated content to foster community participation.

8. Quality Control:

- **Proofreading and Editing:** Prioritize quality control by proofreading and editing your content for grammar, spelling, and clarity. Error-free content enhances professionalism.
- **Fact-Checking:** Ensure that any statistics, data, or claims in your content are accurate and supported

by credible sources.

9. Testing and Optimization:

- **A/B Testing:** Experiment with different content elements, such as headlines, visuals, and calls to action, through A/B testing to determine what resonates best with your audience.
- **Analytics Review:** Regularly review content analytics to assess performance. Identify high-performing content and replicate its success in future pieces.

By implementing these content creation strategies, you can not only produce content that addresses your audience's needs but also create a well-rounded content strategy that engages, educates, and drives conversions. Remember that content creation is an iterative process, and ongoing refinement based on audience feedback and data analysis is essential for sustained success in affiliate marketing.

4.2.3 Writing Effective Product Reviews

Product reviews are a linchpin of affiliate marketing, offering a powerful way to connect with your audience and influence their purchasing decisions. Crafting effective product reviews is both an art and a science, requiring a delicate balance of transparency, persuasion, and authenticity. In this section, we'll delve into the art of crafting compelling product reviews, providing you with a step-by-step guide to writing honest and persuasive reviews that captivate your audience and drive conversions.

Step 1: Choose the Right Products

- **Select Relevant Products:** Choose products that are relevant to your niche and align with the interests and needs of your audience. Promoting products that resonate with your target demographic enhances the effectiveness of your reviews.

- **Consider Your Audience:** Think about your audience's preferences, budget, and pain points. Select products that address their specific concerns and offer value.

Step 2: Thorough Product Research

- **Use the Product:** Whenever possible, use the product yourself to gain firsthand experience. This allows you to provide genuine insights and address real-world pros and cons.
- **Research Extensively:** If you can't personally use the product, conduct thorough research. Study the product specifications, features, customer reviews, and expert opinions to gather comprehensive information.

Step 3: Structuring Your Review

- **Engaging Introduction:** Start with an engaging introduction that highlights the product's significance, its relevance to your audience, and the problem it solves.
- **Clear Product Presentation:** Provide clear and concise information about the product, including its name, brand, key features, and specifications. Include high-quality images or videos to visually showcase the product.
- **User Experience:** Share your personal experience with the product, discussing how it met or exceeded your expectations. Be specific about the benefits it offers.
- **Pros and Cons:** Offer a balanced assessment of the product's strengths and weaknesses. Being transparent about both positive and negative aspects enhances your credibility.
- **Comparison:** If applicable, compare the product with similar alternatives in the market. Highlight

what sets it apart and why it may be the better choice.

Step 4: Authenticity and Transparency

- **Honesty:** Be honest and objective in your assessment. Your audience values authenticity, and dishonesty can damage your reputation.
- **Disclosure:** Clearly disclose your affiliate relationship with the product or brand. Transparency builds trust with your audience.

Step 5: Addressing Common Questions

- **Anticipate Questions:** Think about the questions your audience might have about the product and address them in your review. This demonstrates that you understand their concerns.
- **User Feedback:** Incorporate user feedback and testimonials when relevant. Real-life experiences from other customers can bolster your review.

Step 6: Call to Action

- **Clear Recommendations:** Provide a clear and confident recommendation based on your assessment. Indicate whether you recommend the product and why.
- **Affiliate Links:** Include affiliate links strategically within your review, making them easily accessible to readers who are ready to make a purchase.

Step 7: Engage With Your Audience

- **Encourage Comments:** Encourage readers to leave comments, ask questions, and share their experiences with the product. Engage with them in the comments section to foster interaction.

Step 8: Continuously Update Your Reviews

- **Stay Current:** Keep your reviews up to date, especially for products that undergo changes or updates.

Outdated information can lead to confusion and distrust.

Step 9: Monitor Performance
- **Analyze Analytics:** Regularly analyze the performance of your product reviews. Track metrics like click-through rates, conversion rates, and user engagement to assess their effectiveness.
- **Iterate and Improve:** Based on your analytics, make iterative improvements to your reviews. Experiment with different approaches and elements to optimize conversion rates.

Writing effective product reviews is an art that requires a blend of product knowledge, transparency, and persuasive writing. By following this step-by-step guide and continually refining your approach, you can create reviews that not only inform but also influence your audience's buying decisions. Remember that building trust with your readers is paramount, and consistently delivering honest and valuable reviews will solidify your reputation as a trusted affiliate marketer.

4.2.4 Visual and Multimedia Content

In the realm of affiliate marketing, the saying "a picture is worth a thousand words" couldn't be more accurate. Visual and multimedia content play a pivotal role in engaging your audience, conveying information effectively, and driving conversions. In this section, we'll explore the immense importance of visual and multimedia content in affiliate marketing and provide you with insights on creating engaging images, videos, and infographics that captivate your audience and enhance your affiliate marketing strategy.

The Importance of Visual and Multimedia Content:

Visual and multimedia content, such as images, videos, and infographics, serve as powerful tools to complement your written content. Here's why they matter:

1. Capturing Attention:

- **Visual Appeal:** Visual content grabs your audience's attention quickly, making a strong first impression. It can entice users to engage with your content when they might otherwise scroll past.

2. Enhancing Understanding:

- **Complex Concepts:** Visuals simplify complex information. They can help explain intricate features, processes, or concepts related to the products or services you're promoting.
- **Product Demonstrations:** Videos and images allow you to demonstrate how products work or how they benefit users. This is especially valuable for tech gadgets, software, or any product that benefits from visual demonstration.

3. Improving Engagement:

- **Shareability:** Visual content is highly shareable on social media platforms. Users are more likely to share striking images or informative infographics, expanding your content's reach.
- **Increased Dwell Time:** Engaging multimedia content can keep users on your website longer, reducing bounce rates and improving your site's overall performance.

4. Building Trust:

- **Credibility:** High-quality visuals enhance the perceived credibility of your content and your brand. They convey professionalism and attention to detail.
- **Showcasing Products:** Visuals provide a tangible view of the products you're promoting, making them more real and relatable to your audience.

Creating Engaging Visual and Multimedia Content:

Now that we understand the importance of visual and multimedia content, let's explore how to create content that truly engages your audience:

1. **High-Quality Images:**
   - **Resolution:** Ensure your images are of high resolution and quality. Blurry or pixelated images detract from the professionalism of your content.
   - **Relevance:** Use images that are directly relevant to the content they accompany. They should enhance the user's understanding or support the message.

2. **Engaging Videos:**
   - **Scripting:** Plan your videos with a clear script or outline. Well-structured videos are more effective in conveying information.
   - **Editing:** Invest time in editing your videos. Trim unnecessary segments, add captions, and enhance audio quality.
   - **Thumbnail:** Design eye-catching video thumbnails to encourage clicks and views.

3. **Informative Infographics:**
   - **Data Presentation:** Use infographics to present data, statistics, or comparisons. Visualize information in a way that's easy to understand.
   - **Design:** Pay attention to the design of your infographics. They should be visually appealing and easy to follow.

4. **Consistency:**
   - **Brand Elements:** Maintain consistency in visual elements like color schemes, fonts, and logos. This reinforces your brand identity.

5. **Mobile Optimization:**
   - **Responsive Design:** Ensure that your visual content

is mobile-friendly. Many users access content on smartphones, and mobile optimization is crucial.

6. **Testing and Feedback:**
   - **User Feedback:** Gather feedback from your audience regarding your visual content. What resonates with them? What do they find engaging?
   - **A/B Testing:** Experiment with different visual elements to see what drives better engagement and conversions.

Visual and multimedia content should be an integral part of your affiliate marketing strategy. They not only enhance the overall user experience but also contribute significantly to the success of your promotional efforts. Invest in creating engaging visuals, and you'll find that they can be the catalyst for increased engagement, higher click-through rates, and ultimately, more conversions. Remember that visual content is a dynamic field, so stay updated with current design trends and technologies to keep your affiliate marketing strategy fresh and effective.

4.3 Promoting Your Affiliate Creations

In the ever-evolving world of affiliate marketing, success relies on not only crafting compelling content but also on the art of effective promotion. Here, we delve into strategies and techniques to ensure your affiliate creations reach their intended audience, amplifying your content's visibility, driving targeted traffic, and ultimately boosting your affiliate earnings.

4.3.1 Content Promotion Strategies

In the vast landscape of digital marketing, creating outstanding affiliate content is merely the first step towards success. To truly thrive as an affiliate marketer, you need to master the crucial art of content promotion. This section is dedicated to unraveling the necessity of promoting your affiliate content and exploring diverse methods to ensure your creations reach a wider audience, driving traffic, engagement, and ultimately, conversions.

Understanding the Necessity of Content Promotion:

Creating excellent affiliate content is undeniably important, but it's only valuable when it reaches the right eyes. Here's why content promotion is essential:

1. Reaching a Wider Audience:

- **Expanded Reach:** Promotion strategies extend your content's reach, ensuring it doesn't remain buried in the vast expanse of the internet.
- **Targeted Exposure:** Effective promotion allows you to get your content in front of the audience most likely to convert, increasing your chances of success.

2. Boosting Visibility:

- **Search Engine Rankings:** Promotion can improve your content's search engine rankings, making it more discoverable to users actively seeking information in your niche.
- **Social Engagement:** Promotion through social media encourages likes, shares, and comments, which can lead to increased visibility among users' networks.

3. Establishing Authority:

- **Consistent Presence:** Frequent promotion reinforces your presence in your niche, positioning you as an authority figure and building trust with your audience.
- **Engagement and Interaction:** Regular interaction with your audience through promotion fosters a sense of community and loyalty.

Effective Content Promotion Strategies:

Now, let's delve into the methods that will amplify the reach of your affiliate content:

1. Search Engine Optimization (SEO):

- **Keyword Optimization:** Implement SEO best practices by optimizing your content with relevant keywords. This helps your content rank higher in search engine results pages (SERPs).
- **Quality Backlinks:** Acquire quality backlinks from reputable websites to boost your content's authority and search engine ranking.

2. Social Media Promotion:

- **Leverage Platforms:** Share your content on social media platforms relevant to your niche. Craft engaging posts and use appropriate hashtags to reach a broader audience.
- **Engage with Followers:** Actively engage with your social media followers by responding to comments, asking questions, and encouraging discussions related to your content.

3. Email Marketing:

- **Subscriber List:** Build an email subscriber list of individuals interested in your niche. Send newsletters featuring your latest content, promotions, and affiliate recommendations.
- **Personalization:** Tailor your emails to individual subscribers, personalizing content based on their preferences and behavior.

4. Paid Advertising:

- **Pay-Per-Click (PPC):** Invest in PPC advertising campaigns on platforms like Google Ads or social media to promote your content to a targeted audience.
- **Sponsored Content:** Consider sponsoring your content on platforms that offer this option, ensuring it reaches a broader audience.

5. Content Syndication:

- **Publishing Platforms:** Share your content on platforms like Medium, LinkedIn Pulse, or industry-specific forums to reach a wider readership.
- **Guest Posting:** Write guest posts for reputable websites within your niche, including links to your affiliate content.

6. Influencer Collaborations:

- **Leverage Influencers:** Partner with influencers in your niche who can promote your content to their engaged followers.
- **Affiliate Partnerships:** Collaborate with fellow affiliates to cross-promote each other's content and products.

7. Analytics and Iteration:

- **Monitor Performance:** Regularly analyze the performance of your promotion efforts using analytics tools. Identify what's working and what needs improvement.
- **Iterate and Optimize:** Based on your analysis, refine your promotion strategies to maximize their effectiveness over time.

Effective content promotion is the bridge that connects your affiliate creations to your target audience. It's the key to unlocking the true potential of your affiliate marketing endeavors. By combining the power of SEO, social media, email marketing, paid advertising, and other strategies, you can ensure that your affiliate content not only stands out in a crowded digital landscape but also drives meaningful engagement and conversions, solidifying your success as an affiliate marketer. Remember that persistence and adaptability are key; keep refining your promotion tactics as you learn more about what resonates with your audience.

4.3.2 Building an Email List

In the dynamic realm of affiliate marketing, one strategy stands out as a cornerstone of success: email marketing. It's not just a tool; it's a direct line of communication with your audience, making it a potent asset for promoting your affiliate creations. In this section, we'll delve into the pivotal role of email marketing in affiliate promotion and offer you valuable guidance on building and nurturing an email subscriber list that will be the engine driving your affiliate business forward.

Understanding the Role of Email Marketing:

Email marketing isn't just about sending promotional messages; it's about building meaningful relationships with your audience.
Here's why it's a game-changer in affiliate promotion:

1. Direct Communication:
- **Personal Connection:** Email provides a direct and personal channel to connect with your audience. It's a one-on-one conversation in their inbox.
- **Customized Content:** With email, you can send customized content tailored to each subscriber's interests, preferences, and behavior.

2. Relationship Building:
- **Trust and Credibility:** Consistent and valuable emails build trust and credibility over time, making your audience more receptive to your recommendations.
- **Long-term Engagement:** Email allows you to engage with your audience over the long term, fostering loyalty and repeat business.

3. Conversion Power:
- **Conversion Rates:** Email marketing often boasts higher conversion rates compared to other channels. When done right, it can drive affiliate sales effectively.
- **Promotion Versatility:** You can use email to promote

various affiliate products, share blog posts, offer exclusive discounts, and more.

Building and Nurturing an Email Subscriber List:

Now that we've established the importance of email marketing, let's explore how to start and grow your email subscriber list:

1. Create Valuable Content:
- **Incentive:** Offer an incentive like a free e-book, discount, or valuable resource in exchange for subscribers' email addresses.
- **Quality Content:** Ensure your website and content are of high quality. Visitors are more likely to subscribe if they find your content valuable.

2. Opt-in Forms:
- **Placement:** Strategically place opt-in forms on your website, including pop-ups, embedded forms, and dedicated landing pages.
- **Clarity:** Clearly explain the benefits of subscribing, such as receiving exclusive offers or staying updated with your niche.

3. Segmentation:
- **Data Collection:** Collect additional data during sign-up to segment your list effectively. This allows you to send targeted content.
- **Behavior Tracking:** Track user behavior and tailor your emails based on how subscribers interact with your content.

4. Consistent Communication:
- **Regular Emails:** Maintain a consistent email schedule, whether it's weekly newsletters, bi-weekly updates, or other intervals.
- **Value First:** Prioritize providing value in your emails. Educational content, tips, and insights keep

subscribers engaged.

5. Engagement and Interactivity:

- **Ask for Feedback:** Encourage subscribers to provide feedback, ask questions, or suggest topics they'd like to see covered.
- **Surveys and Polls:** Use surveys and polls to gather opinions and preferences, tailoring your content accordingly.

6. A/B Testing:

- **Subject Lines:** Experiment with different subject lines, email formats, and content types to discover what resonates best with your audience.
- **Timing:** Test sending emails at different times and days to determine when your audience is most receptive.

7. Compliance and Privacy:

- **Compliance:** Ensure that your email marketing practices comply with relevant data protection laws, such as GDPR or CAN-SPAM.
- **Privacy:** Assure subscribers that their data is safe and that you won't share it with third parties.

Building and nurturing an email subscriber list is an ongoing process that requires patience and dedication. It's an investment in a valuable asset that can propel your affiliate marketing business to new heights. As you grow your list and send targeted, valuable content, you'll find that email marketing isn't just about promotion; it's about fostering genuine connections and building a community of engaged subscribers who trust your recommendations and eagerly await your emails.

4.3.3 Leveraging Social Media

In the fast-paced world of affiliate marketing, social media is your dynamic playground for promoting affiliate products, engaging with your audience, and driving traffic to your affiliate content. This section will unveil the secrets of effectively using social media platforms to supercharge your affiliate marketing efforts. Get ready to discover strategies for building a loyal following, engaging with your followers, and harnessing the immense power of social media to boost your affiliate earnings.

Effectively Using Social Media for Affiliate Marketing:

Social media platforms are bustling hubs of activity, making them fertile grounds for affiliate promotion. Here's how to harness their potential:

1. Platform Selection:

- **Know Your Audience:** Understand your target audience's preferred social media platforms. Focus your efforts on the platforms where they're most active.
- **Diversify:** While focusing on key platforms is essential, consider maintaining a presence on multiple platforms to reach a broader audience.

2. Content Creation:

- **Quality over Quantity:** Create high-quality content that resonates with your audience. Focus on providing value, whether it's through informative posts, engaging visuals, or entertaining videos.
- **Visual Appeal:** Visual content, such as images, videos, and infographics, often performs exceptionally well on social media. Invest in eye-catching visuals.

3. Consistency and Frequency:

- **Regular Posting:** Maintain a consistent posting schedule to keep your audience engaged. Consistency builds trust and keeps your brand top of mind.
- **Engagement Timing:** Post at times when your target

audience is most active on the platform. Analytics tools can help determine optimal posting times.

4. Engagement Strategies:

- **Respond Promptly:** Interact with comments and messages from your followers promptly. Engage in conversations and answer questions.
- **User-Generated Content:** Encourage users to create content related to your affiliate products and share it on their profiles. This not only promotes the products but also leverages their existing followers.

5. Hashtags and Keywords:

- **Strategic Use:** Incorporate relevant hashtags and keywords in your posts to increase discoverability. Research trending hashtags within your niche.
- **Brand Recognition:** Create a unique hashtag associated with your brand or niche to foster community engagement.

6. Promotions and Contests:

- **Giveaways:** Host giveaways or contests that require participants to engage with your content, follow your profile, or tag friends. This can rapidly increase your follower count and engagement.
- **Discounts and Promo Codes:** Share exclusive affiliate discounts and promo codes with your followers. Limited-time offers can create a sense of urgency.

7. Analytics and Optimization:

- **Performance Analysis:** Use social media analytics tools to track the performance of your posts and campaigns. Analyze which content resonates best with your audience.
- **Adjust and Refine:** Based on your analytics, adjust

your social media strategy. Refine your content, posting times, and engagement strategies to optimize results.

8. Paid Advertising:

- **Boosted Posts:** Consider investing in paid advertising to reach a larger, targeted audience. Platforms like Facebook and Instagram offer ad campaigns tailored to your goals.

9. Influencer Collaborations:

- **Partnerships:** Collaborate with influencers in your niche for sponsored posts or affiliate partnerships. Their endorsement can significantly impact your affiliate sales.

Social media is a dynamic and ever-evolving landscape, making it a powerhouse for affiliate marketing. By crafting engaging content, fostering meaningful interactions, and strategically using platforms and features, you can tap into the vast potential of social media to amplify your affiliate earnings. Remember that success on social media is built on authenticity and genuine connections, so stay true to your brand, provide value, and engage with your audience wholeheartedly. With dedication and creativity, your social media presence can become a formidable force in your affiliate marketing strategy.

4.3.4 Analyzing Content Performance

In the ever-evolving world of affiliate marketing, knowledge is power, and data is your most potent ally. This section will illuminate the critical importance of tracking and analyzing your content's performance. We'll dive into the tools and metrics that will help you measure your success, optimize your strategies, and ensure your affiliate marketing endeavors remain on the path to prosperity.

Understanding the Importance of Tracking and Analysis:

Tracking and analyzing content performance might not be the most glamorous part of affiliate marketing, but it's undeniably one of the most crucial. Here's why it's a game-changer:

1. Informed Decision-Making:

- **Data-Driven Insights:** Analyzing performance data provides insights into what's working and what's not. It empowers you to make informed decisions about your affiliate strategies.
- **Optimization:** By understanding what resonates with your audience, you can optimize your content and promotion efforts for better results.

2. Goal Achievement:

- **Progress Tracking:** Metrics help you track progress toward your affiliate marketing goals, whether it's increasing traffic, click-through rates, or conversion rates.
- **Identifying Weaknesses:** Data analysis reveals weak points in your strategy that need attention, enabling you to plug leaks and improve performance.

3. Resource Allocation:

- **Efficient Resource Allocation:** Analyzing content performance guides you in allocating your time and resources where they'll yield the highest return on investment.
- **Budget Optimization:** It allows you to optimize your advertising spend, focusing on campaigns and channels that deliver the best results.

Introducing Tools and Metrics for Measuring Success:

Now, let's explore the essential tools and metrics that will help you measure your affiliate marketing success:

1. Google Analytics:

- **Traffic Sources:** Track where your website traffic is coming from, whether it's organic search, social media, or referrals.
- **Conversion Tracking:** Set up conversion goals to monitor affiliate sales and other crucial actions on your site.

2. Affiliate Dashboards:

- **Click-Through Rate (CTR):** Measure how many clicks your affiliate links receive compared to the total number of impressions.
- **Conversion Rate:** Calculate the percentage of clicks that lead to a conversion, such as a sale or sign-up.
- **Earnings Per Click (EPC):** Evaluate the average earnings generated per click on your affiliate links.

3. Social Media Insights:

- **Engagement Metrics:** Track likes, shares, comments, and follower growth to assess the performance of your social media promotion efforts.
- **Click Data:** Most social platforms provide insights into the performance of your shared affiliate links.

4. Email Marketing Tools:

- **Open Rates:** Measure how many recipients open your affiliate marketing emails.
- **Click-Through Rates:** Analyze the percentage of email recipients who clicked on your affiliate links.
- **Conversion Tracking:** Monitor the actions taken by subscribers after clicking on affiliate links in your emails.

5. SEO Tools:

- **Keyword Rankings:** Track the ranking of your affiliate-related content for specific keywords in search engine results.

- **Backlink Analysis:** Evaluate the quality and quantity of backlinks to your affiliate content.

6. A/B Testing Tools:

- **Split Testing:** Use A/B testing to compare different versions of content or ad campaigns to determine which performs better.

7. Heatmaps and User Behavior Analysis:

- **Heatmaps:** Visualize how users interact with your website and where they click or scroll the most.
- **User Behavior Analysis:** Understand how visitors navigate your site and where they drop off.

8. Feedback and Surveys:

- **User Feedback:** Collect feedback from your audience to understand their preferences and pain points.
- **Surveys:** Use surveys to gather insights on how to improve your affiliate content and strategies.

9. Affiliate Network Reports:

- **Commission Reports:** Monitor your earnings, clicks, and conversions through your affiliate network's reporting dashboard.

Effective analysis isn't a one-time endeavor but an ongoing process. Regularly review your performance data, identify trends, and make adjustments accordingly. By embracing data-driven decision-making, you'll be better equipped to fine-tune your affiliate marketing strategies, seize opportunities, and ensure your efforts yield the maximum return on investment. Remember that in affiliate marketing, knowledge truly is power, and tracking your performance is the compass guiding you toward success.

CHAPTER 5: GENERATING TARGETED TRAFFIC

In this pivotal chapter, we'll delve into the art and science of driving the right audience to your affiliate content. Discover strategies and tactics that will not only increase traffic but ensure that it's laser-focused on the individuals most likely to convert, ultimately maximizing your affiliate marketing success. Get ready to explore the metrics that matter and the methods that make a difference.

5.1 The Traffic Game

Welcome to the world of affiliate marketing traffic, where your website's lifeblood flows through the visitors it attracts. In this section, we'll explore the dynamics of website traffic and why it's the driving force behind successful affiliate marketing. Learn how to strategically attract and engage your ideal audience, setting the stage for affiliate marketing triumphs.

5.1.1 Understanding the Traffic Landscape

In the realm of affiliate marketing, website traffic is the heartbeat of your online presence. It's not just about numbers; it's about the quality and relevance of the visitors your website attracts. In this section, we'll embark on a journey to grasp the intricacies of the traffic landscape, unraveling its profound significance in achieving affiliate marketing goals.

Introducing the Concept of Website Traffic:

Website traffic, in its simplest form, refers to the number of visitors who come to your website. However, it's crucial to understand that not all traffic is created equal. It can be categorized into various types:

1. **Organic Traffic:** Visitors who find your website through search engines like Google. This traffic is often highly relevant because it's driven by user intent.
2. **Referral Traffic:** Visitors who arrive at your site via links from other websites. The quality of referral traffic depends on the relevance and authority of the referring site.
3. **Direct Traffic:** Visitors who type your website's URL directly into their browser. This can include loyal followers or people who have heard about your site through other means.
4. **Social Traffic:** Visitors who discover your website through social media platforms. Social traffic can be highly engaged if your content resonates with your social media audience.
5. **Paid Traffic:** Visitors acquired through paid advertising campaigns. The quality of paid traffic depends on your targeting and ad copy.

Significance in Achieving Affiliate Goals:

Understanding the concept of website traffic is the first step in recognizing its paramount importance in the affiliate marketing landscape. Here's why it matters:

1. **Audience Reach:** Traffic is the conduit through which you reach your target audience. Without visitors, your affiliate content remains unseen and unheard.

2. **Conversion Potential:** The more targeted and relevant your traffic is, the higher the likelihood of conversions.

Quality traffic increases the chances of visitors taking desired actions, such as making a purchase through your affiliate links.

3. **Revenue Generation:** For affiliate marketers, revenue is often directly tied to traffic. More traffic means more opportunities for affiliate clicks and conversions, ultimately leading to increased earnings.

4. **Building Authority:** A website with substantial, relevant traffic is often seen as authoritative and trustworthy in its niche. This perception can enhance your affiliate marketing efforts, as users are more likely to trust recommendations from credible sources.

5. **Data Insights:** Analyzing your website's traffic provides valuable insights into your audience's behavior, preferences, and pain points. This data is instrumental in refining your affiliate strategies.

6. **Scaling Possibilities:** As your traffic grows, so do your affiliate marketing possibilities. With a larger audience base, you can explore various affiliate programs, niches, and revenue streams.

7. **Long-term Sustainability:** Sustainable affiliate success often hinges on consistent traffic. A steady flow of visitors ensures your affiliate content remains relevant and profitable over time.

In summary, website traffic is not just a numerical metric; it's the life force of your affiliate marketing journey. Understanding the nuances of the traffic landscape and its role in achieving affiliate goals is a fundamental step in your path to affiliate marketing triumphs. As we delve deeper into this chapter, we'll uncover strategies and tactics to not only increase traffic but also ensure it's precisely the audience you need to propel your affiliate endeavors to new heights.

5.1.2 Sources of Web Traffic

In the dynamic landscape of affiliate marketing, understanding the diverse sources of web traffic is akin to having a palette of colors at your disposal to create a masterpiece. Each traffic source brings its unique hues, allowing you to paint your affiliate marketing canvas with precision. In this section, we'll delve into these sources, from the organic flow of search engines to the targeted precision of paid traffic and the referrals from other digital domains.

Organic Traffic: The Power of Search Engines

Pros:

1. **Relevance:** Organic traffic comes from users actively searching for information related to your content or niche, making it highly relevant.
2. **Sustainability:** Once your content ranks well in search results, it can provide a consistent stream of traffic over time.
3. **Cost-Effective:** Unlike paid traffic, organic traffic doesn't require ongoing financial investment.

Cons:

1. **Time-Intensive:** Achieving high rankings in search engine results takes time and effort.
2. **Competition:** Depending on your niche, you may face stiff competition for top search engine positions.
3. **Algorithm Changes:** Search engines frequently update their algorithms, which can impact your rankings.

Paid Traffic: Precision with a Price Tag

Pros:

1. **Speed:** Paid traffic campaigns can quickly generate visitors to your site.
2. **Targeting:** You can precisely target your audience based on demographics, interests, and behavior.
3. **Control:** You have full control over your ad campaigns,

budgets, and ad creatives.

Cons:

1. **Cost:** Paid traffic can become expensive, especially if not managed carefully.
2. **Learning Curve:** Effectively managing paid traffic campaigns requires knowledge and optimization skills.
3. **Ad Blindness:** Users are becoming increasingly ad-savvy and may ignore or block ads.

Referral Traffic: The Power of Recommendations

Pros:

1. **Trust:** Referral traffic often comes from trusted sources, which can enhance your credibility.
2. **Quality:** Visitors referred from relevant websites are more likely to engage with your content.
3. **Networking:** Building relationships with other websites can lead to ongoing referral traffic.

Cons:

1. **Dependency:** Relying solely on referral traffic can leave you vulnerable if referral sources change their linking strategies.
2. **Variable Quality:** Not all referral traffic is created equal. The quality can vary depending on the referring website.
3. **Maintenance:** Building and maintaining referral relationships requires time and effort.

Direct Traffic: The Familiar Path

Pros:

1. **Loyalty:** Direct traffic often includes loyal followers who are familiar with your brand.
2. **Consistency:** It provides a steady stream of visitors who know your website and its content.
3. **Word-of-Mouth:** Direct traffic can result from word-of-mouth recommendations.

Cons:

1. **Limited Growth:** Relying solely on direct traffic may limit your ability to expand your audience.
2. **Stagnation:** Without efforts to attract new visitors, direct traffic may plateau over time.
3. **Dependency:** Your traffic may be largely dependent on a loyal but finite audience.

Social Traffic: Riding the Social Wave

Pros:

1. **Engagement:** Social media platforms enable direct engagement with your audience.
2. **Amplification:** Viral content on social media can lead to a rapid increase in traffic.
3. **Targeting:** Social media ads offer precise targeting options.

Cons:

1. **Algorithm Changes:** Social media algorithms frequently evolve, affecting organic reach.
2. **Time-Intensive:** Managing social media profiles and creating engaging content can be time-consuming.
3. **Paid Advertising Costs:** While effective, social media advertising can become costly.

Understanding the pros and cons of these traffic sources is essential for creating a well-rounded affiliate marketing strategy. In practice, a combination of these sources often yields the best results. As we delve deeper into this chapter, we'll explore strategies for optimizing each traffic source to maximize its potential and drive targeted traffic to your affiliate content.

5.1.3 The Role of Traffic in Conversion

Imagine your affiliate marketing journey as a bustling marketplace. The visitors to your website are the shoppers, and each interaction they have with your content is a step closer to making a purchase through your affiliate links. In this section, we'll unravel the intricate relationship between traffic, both in terms of quantity and quality, and its profound impact on affiliate conversion rates. To illustrate this relationship, we'll journey through real-world examples that showcase the correlation between traffic and earnings.

Traffic Quantity: The Volume Game

First, let's address the quantity aspect of traffic. It's often said that "more is better," but is this always the case in affiliate marketing?

Scenario 1: Low Traffic Volume

Imagine you have a website in a highly specialized niche with low search volume. You're attracting a modest 500 visitors per month, but these visitors are extremely targeted and passionate about your niche. Due to the niche's exclusivity, the affiliate products you promote perfectly match their interests and needs.

In this scenario, despite the low traffic volume, your conversion rates are high. Why? Because your visitors are genuinely interested in your content, and the affiliate products you recommend align seamlessly with their preferences. Your earnings per visitor are substantial, and your affiliate marketing efforts are profitable.

Scenario 2: High Traffic Volume

Now, consider a different scenario. You've ventured into a broader niche that attracts a massive amount of traffic—let's say 100,000 visitors per month. However, this niche is highly competitive, and your content faces fierce competition from established players.

In this case, your conversion rates may be lower compared to the previous scenario. The sheer volume of visitors doesn't guarantee higher earnings per visitor. You're battling for attention in a crowded marketplace, and your affiliate products might not resonate as strongly with your audience.

Traffic Quality: The Relevance Factor

Now, let's delve into the quality aspect of traffic. Quality traffic comprises visitors who are not just passing through but are genuinely interested in your content and the affiliate products you promote.

Scenario 3: High-Quality Traffic

In this scenario, you've mastered the art of targeting and attracting high-quality traffic. Your content is optimized for search engines, and you rank well for relevant keywords. You've built a loyal social media following, and your email subscribers are genuinely interested in your recommendations.

Despite having a moderate traffic volume—let's say 10,000 visitors per month—your conversion rates soar. Your audience trusts your recommendations, and the affiliate products you promote cater precisely to their needs. Your earnings per visitor are impressive, and you're reaping the rewards of quality traffic.

Scenario 4: Low-Quality Traffic

Contrast this with a scenario where you're driving a massive amount of traffic—perhaps 500,000 visitors per month—yet the quality is lacking. Many of these visitors are accidental or uninterested in your niche. They bounce quickly from your site, rarely engaging with your content or clicking on your affiliate links.

Here, despite the astronomical traffic volume, your conversion rates plummet. Your earnings per visitor are meager because your audience lacks genuine interest in your content and the affiliate products you promote.

The Conversion Equation: Quality + Quantity

So, what does this all mean for your affiliate marketing

endeavors?

The key takeaway is that both traffic quantity and quality play pivotal roles in the affiliate conversion equation. While a high volume of traffic can be advantageous, it must be complemented by quality. Quality traffic comprises individuals genuinely interested in your niche and recommendations.

Ideally, you want to strike a balance between the two. Attract a sufficient volume of quality traffic that aligns with your niche, engages with your content, and converts through your affiliate links. This balance is where the magic happens—the sweet spot where traffic fuels conversions, and conversions fuel earnings.

As you embark on your affiliate marketing journey, remember that it's not just about numbers or the sheer volume of traffic. It's about cultivating an audience that values your content and trusts your recommendations. In the chapters ahead, we'll explore strategies to optimize both the quantity and quality of your traffic, ensuring your affiliate marketing efforts are poised for success.

5.2 Attracting Your Ideal Audience

Welcome to the heart of affiliate marketing success - attracting your ideal audience. In this section, we'll delve into strategies and tactics to magnetize the precise audience that resonates with your niche and converts into loyal affiliates. Get ready to discover the art of targeted attraction that will elevate your affiliate marketing game.

5.2.1 Defining Your Target Audience

In the sprawling landscape of affiliate marketing, one of the fundamental pillars of success is the precise understanding and definition of your target audience. Imagine this process as the sculptor chiseling away excess stone to reveal the exquisite masterpiece hidden within. In this section, we'll emphasize the critical significance of audience segmentation in affiliate marketing and provide you with actionable methods for not only identifying but also defining your ideal audience.

The Importance of Audience Segmentation: Precision Matters

Picture this: you have a treasure chest filled with valuable affiliate products and services. Each product is uniquely suited to cater to specific needs and desires. However, to unlock the riches within, you must handpick the individuals most likely to find value in what you offer.

This is where audience segmentation comes into play. It's the process of dividing your broader audience into distinct, well-defined segments based on characteristics, interests, and behaviors. Why is this crucial?

- **Relevance:** By understanding the specific needs and preferences of each segment, you can tailor your affiliate marketing efforts to resonate deeply with them.
- **Personalization:** Personalized content and recommendations have a significantly higher impact on conversion rates than generic messaging.
- **Efficiency:** Instead of casting a wide net and hoping for the best, you focus your efforts and resources on the segments most likely to convert.

Methods for Identifying and Defining Your Ideal Audience

Now, let's explore methods for identifying and defining your ideal audience:

1. **Market Research:** Begin with comprehensive market research within your niche, including competitor analysis and trend assessment. This research provides critical insights into your niche's landscape, helping you pinpoint opportunities and gaps.
2. **Customer Surveys:** Conduct surveys among your

existing audience to gather insights into their demographics, preferences, and pain points. These surveys help you directly connect with your audience, uncover their needs, and refine your targeting strategies.

3. **Analytics Tools:** Leverage web analytics to understand your current audience's behavior and preferences. Analyze data on page views, click-through rates, and user demographics to fine-tune your content and promotional efforts.

4. **Social Media Listening:** Monitor niche-related social media platforms to engage with your target audience and grasp their needs and challenges. By actively participating in conversations and gathering feedback, you can tailor your content and promotions to better serve your audience.

5. **Persona Creation:** Develop detailed audience personas representing your ideal segments, including demographics, interests, and behaviors. These personas serve as a clear reference for crafting content and campaigns that resonate with specific audience groups.

6. **Keyword Research:** Perform keyword research to discover what your audience is searching for, helping you craft relevant content. Keywords provide valuable insights into the topics, questions, and concerns that matter most to your audience.

7. **Affiliate Product Alignment:** Consider the target audience of the affiliate products or services you promote to align your efforts. Ensure that your content and promotions cater to the needs and interests of the same audience that the products serve.

8. **Competitor Analysis:** Analyze your competitors' audience targeting to identify gaps or opportunities for your content. By understanding the segments your competitors may overlook, you can position yourself

effectively.

9. **A/B Testing:** Experiment with different content, messaging, and offers to refine your understanding of specific audience segments. A/B testing allows you to fine-tune your strategies based on real-time performance data and audience feedback.

In the world of affiliate marketing, precision matters more than volume. Defining your target audience with accuracy enables you to create content and recommendations that strike a chord with the right people. As we journey further into this chapter, we'll explore strategies for not only attracting your ideal audience but also nurturing their engagement and conversions, ensuring that your affiliate marketing efforts are both effective and rewarding.

5.2.2 Content Tailored to Your Audience

Imagine you're hosting a dinner party, and your guests have diverse tastes and dietary preferences. To ensure everyone enjoys the meal, you meticulously plan a menu that caters to each guest's specific cravings. In the world of affiliate marketing, your audience is your guest list, and your content is the menu. It's essential to craft content that not only resonates but also captivates your target audience. In this section, we'll delve into the critical need for content tailored to your audience and provide you with a repertoire of strategies for creating content that addresses their pain points and interests.

The Audience-Content Connection: A Harmonious Symphony

Before we dive into strategies, let's dissect the fundamental link between your audience and your content:

1. **Relevance:** Content that aligns with your audience's needs and interests is more likely to capture their attention. It's like speaking their language.
2. **Engagement:** When your audience finds content that

directly addresses their pain points or piques their interests, they are more likely to engage with it, whether through reading, sharing, or clicking on affiliate links.

3. **Trust:** Tailored content positions you as an authority in your niche. When your audience perceives you as a trusted source of valuable information, they are more likely to act on your recommendations.

Strategies for Tailoring Content to Your Audience

Now, let's explore effective strategies for crafting content that speaks directly to your target audience:

1. Audience Personas: Remember those detailed audience personas we discussed earlier? Use them as your compass. Each piece of content you create should align with one or more of these personas. Consider their demographics, interests, challenges, and preferences.

2. Pain Point Addressing: Identify the pain points or problems your audience faces within your niche. Create content that provides solutions, answers questions, or offers insights into these pain points. For example, if you're in the fitness niche, address common fitness challenges with actionable advice.

3. Educational Content: Position yourself as an educator. Offer tutorials, how-to guides, and informative articles that help your audience learn and grow within your niche. Educational content not only fosters trust but also keeps your audience engaged.

4. Storytelling: Narratives have an incredible power to connect. Share personal anecdotes or stories related to your niche that resonate with your audience. Stories are memorable and relatable.

5. Surveys and Feedback: Don't guess what your audience wants —ask them. Conduct surveys, engage with comments, and seek feedback on your content. Use this input to refine your content strategy.

6. Trend Utilization: Keep an eye on trends within your niche. Create content that capitalizes on these trends. Trend-related content is more likely to grab your audience's attention.

7. Problem-Solution Framework: Structure your content around the problem-solution framework. Begin by addressing a common issue within your niche, then present affiliate products or services as viable solutions.

8. Visual Appeal: Visual elements, such as images, infographics, and videos, can enhance your content's appeal. Visuals are not only engaging but also help explain complex concepts.

9. Consistency: Maintain a consistent tone and style in your content. Your audience should feel a sense of familiarity when consuming your content, which fosters trust.

10. Testing and Adaptation: Use A/B testing to experiment with different content approaches. Analyze performance data to understand what resonates best with your audience, and adapt your content strategy accordingly.

Remember, your content isn't just about selling affiliate products; it's about providing value and building relationships with your audience. The more your content speaks to their needs and interests, the more likely they are to engage, convert, and become loyal affiliates themselves.

As we journey through this chapter, we'll explore additional methods for promoting your tailored content effectively to ensure it reaches your ideal audience and drives desired actions, resulting in a thriving affiliate marketing venture.

5.2.3 SEO and Organic Traffic

Imagine your affiliate marketing website as a hidden gem in a bustling city. It holds invaluable treasures for those who discover it. But how can you ensure your digital gem is found amid the noise of the online world? This is where SEO (Search Engine Optimization) comes into play. In this section, we'll explore the paramount significance of SEO in attracting organic traffic to your affiliate marketing platform and provide you with essential SEO tips to enhance your website's visibility.

The SEO-Powered Elevator: Rising Above the Noise

SEO is the art and science of making your website more visible to search engines like Google, Bing, and Yahoo. Think of search engines as the city's tour guides. When someone in the city (online) is looking for something, they turn to the tour guides for recommendations. If your website is optimized correctly, it's like having your gem displayed prominently in the tour guide's list of must-visit places.

Why is SEO crucial?

1. **Visibility:** SEO helps your website rank higher in search engine results pages (SERPs). The higher you rank, the more likely users will discover your site when searching for relevant keywords.
2. **Credibility:** Websites that appear at the top of search results are often perceived as more credible and trustworthy. SEO can help build your site's authority.
3. **Traffic:** Organic traffic, driven by SEO, is cost-effective and sustainable. It continually brings in visitors without the ongoing expenses of paid advertising.

SEO Tips for Improved Visibility

Now, let's dive into some basic SEO tips to enhance your website's visibility and draw in organic traffic:

1. Keyword Research: Begin by identifying relevant keywords related to your niche. Use keyword research tools to discover which terms your target audience is searching for. Incorporate these keywords naturally into your content.

2. High-Quality Content: Content is king in SEO. Create high-quality, informative, and engaging content that addresses your audience's needs and interests. Google rewards sites with valuable content.

3. On-Page SEO: Optimize your web pages for search engines. This includes using descriptive and keyword-rich titles, headings, and meta descriptions. Ensure your website is mobile-friendly for a better user experience.

4. Quality Backlinks: Build a network of high-quality backlinks from reputable websites within your niche. Backlinks are like endorsements, signaling to search engines that your site is trustworthy.

5. Site Speed: A fast-loading website improves user experience and can positively impact your search engine rankings. Compress images, use a content delivery network (CDN), and choose a reliable hosting provider.

6. User Experience: Create a user-friendly website with easy navigation and clear calls-to-action. A positive user experience can reduce bounce rates and improve SEO.

7. Regular Updates: Keep your content fresh by regularly updating and adding new articles or posts. Google favors websites that provide up-to-date information.

8. Social Signals: While not a direct ranking factor, social media engagement can indirectly influence SEO. Share your content on social platforms to increase visibility and potentially attract backlinks.

9. Schema Markup: Implement schema markup to provide search engines with additional information about your content. This can enhance your search results with rich snippets.

10. Monitor and Adapt: Use analytics tools to monitor your website's performance and track keyword rankings. Adjust your

SEO strategy based on data and trends.

Remember that SEO is an ongoing process. It may take time to see significant results, but the long-term benefits are substantial. By mastering the fundamentals of SEO, you can transform your affiliate marketing website into a highly visible and valuable resource for your target audience, attracting organic traffic and potential affiliates in the process.

5.2.4 Paid Traffic Strategies

Imagine having a magic tap that allows you to instantly direct a stream of eager, targeted visitors to your affiliate marketing platform. While magic taps may not exist, paid advertising comes pretty close. In this section, we'll explore paid traffic strategies, introducing the concept of using paid advertising to attract precisely the right audience. We'll discuss popular platforms like Google Ads and Facebook Ads and provide you with effective strategies for running successful paid campaigns.

Unlocking the Power of Paid Advertising

Paid advertising, often referred to as PPC (Pay-Per-Click) advertising, is like a shortcut to visibility. Instead of waiting for your website to climb the ranks in organic search results, paid ads enable you to put your affiliate offerings in front of your ideal audience right away.

Why consider paid advertising?

1. **Instant Visibility:** With paid ads, your affiliate products or services can appear at the top of search results or within social media feeds almost instantly.
2. **Targeted Reach:** Paid advertising platforms offer robust targeting options. You can define your audience based on demographics, interests, behavior, and more, ensuring your ads reach those most likely to convert.
3. **Measurable ROI:** Paid campaigns provide clear metrics for measuring your return on investment. You can

track clicks, conversions, and revenue, allowing you to fine-tune your strategy.

Effective Strategies for Paid Advertising

Now, let's delve into strategies for running successful paid advertising campaigns:

1. Understand Your Audience: Before you dive into paid advertising, ensure you have a deep understanding of your target audience. Who are they? What are their pain points? What solutions are they seeking? This knowledge will guide your ad targeting.

2. Choose the Right Platform: Different platforms cater to different demographics and interests. Google Ads is excellent for search intent, while Facebook Ads allows you to target users based on their interests and behavior. Pick the platform(s) that align with your audience.

3. Set Clear Goals: Define your campaign objectives. Are you looking to drive website traffic, generate leads, or boost sales? Clear goals will shape your ad creative and strategy.

4. Keyword Research: If you're using search engine advertising like Google Ads, conduct thorough keyword research to identify the terms your audience uses. Craft ads that align with these keywords.

5. Compelling Ad Copy: Your ad copy should be concise, compelling, and relevant. Highlight the value of your affiliate offerings and include a clear call-to-action.

6. Landing Page Optimization: Ensure that the landing pages users reach after clicking your ads are optimized for conversions. They should align with the ad's message and make it easy for users to take the desired action.

7. Budget Management: Set a reasonable budget for your campaigns and monitor spending closely. Start with a modest budget and increase it as you refine your campaigns and see positive results.

8. A/B Testing: Experiment with different ad creatives, headlines, and calls-to-action. A/B testing allows you to identify what resonates most with your audience.

9. Ad Scheduling: Consider the timing of your ads. Schedule them to appear when your target audience is most active and likely to engage.

10. Remarketing: Implement remarketing campaigns to re-engage users who have previously visited your website. Remarketing can be highly effective in nurturing conversions.

11. Analytics and Optimization: Continuously monitor the performance of your paid campaigns. Use analytics data to refine your strategy, adjust budgets, and optimize ad copy.

12. Ad Compliance: Ensure your ads comply with the policies and guidelines of the advertising platform. Non-compliant ads can lead to account suspensions.

Remember that paid advertising requires a balance between investment and return. Start with a clear plan, track your results meticulously, and be prepared to adapt and refine your campaigns based on real-time data. When executed effectively, paid traffic strategies can be a powerful complement to your organic efforts, helping you reach and convert your target audience efficiently.

5.3 Metrics That Matter

Welcome to the world of affiliate marketing metrics that truly matter. We'll dive into the essential data points that will be your compass as you navigate your affiliate marketing journey. These metrics will serve as your guiding stars, helping you assess the effectiveness of your strategies, optimize your efforts, and ultimately steer your affiliate venture toward success.

5.3.1 Key Traffic Metrics

In the digital realm of affiliate marketing, data is more than just numbers; it's your looking glass into the performance of your strategies. Traffic metrics, in particular, act as your early warning system, revealing how your website is faring in the vast sea of the internet. In this section, we'll shine a light on the essential traffic metrics that every affiliate marketer should be intimately familiar with. These metrics not only define the pulse of your website but also offer valuable insights into the quality of your traffic.

Page Views: Imagine your website as a bustling marketplace. Page views represent the foot traffic, indicating how many times visitors have strolled through your virtual stalls. It's a raw number, giving you an idea of your site's popularity and reach.

Unique Visitors: In that bustling marketplace, unique visitors are the individuals who step inside. Unlike page views, which count every interaction, unique visitors measure the distinct individuals engaging with your content. It helps gauge your website's appeal to a broader audience.

Bounce Rate: Imagine a shopper walking into your marketplace, taking a quick look, and leaving without making a purchase. This is akin to what happens when a visitor bounces from your website. The bounce rate tells you the percentage of visitors who land on a page and leave without engaging further. A high bounce rate can signal issues with content quality or relevance.

Session Duration: Picture a visitor exploring your marketplace, spending time in various stalls, and soaking in the experience. Session duration measures how much time visitors spend on your website during a single visit. Longer sessions often indicate engaging content and a deeper interest in your offerings.

Understanding these traffic metrics is like deciphering the language of your audience. Now, let's explore why these metrics matter:

Assessing Traffic Quality: It's not just about the quantity of visitors; it's about the quality. Page views and unique visitors can tell you if you're attracting attention, but bounce rate and session duration reveal if your audience is genuinely engaged. A high bounce rate suggests that visitors aren't finding what they expected or that your content doesn't resonate, while longer session durations indicate content that captivates and holds interest.

Content Optimization: Armed with these metrics, you can fine-tune your content strategy. If you notice a high bounce rate on a particular page, it's a sign that the content may not be meeting visitors' expectations. Consider improving or optimizing that content to reduce bounce rates. Conversely, if you see long session durations on certain pages, identify what makes them compelling and replicate those elements in other parts of your website.

Conversion Potential: Engaged visitors are more likely to convert into leads or customers. By tracking these metrics, you can identify which pages or content types are driving higher-quality traffic. This information can help you focus your affiliate marketing efforts on the areas with the most significant conversion potential.

In the ever-evolving landscape of affiliate marketing, these traffic metrics are your compass, guiding you toward success. They provide the insights needed to tailor your strategies, captivate your audience, and make data-driven decisions that lead to a thriving affiliate venture.

5.3.2 Conversion Tracking: Measuring Success in Affiliate Marketing

Imagine you're on a treasure hunt, and the treasures are conversions – the ultimate goals of your affiliate marketing efforts. Conversion tracking is your treasure map, guiding you through the digital wilderness to uncover the hidden gems. In this section, we'll explore the critical role of conversion tracking in evaluating the effectiveness of your traffic and introduce you to the tools and methods that will help you unearth those valuable conversions.

The Significance of Conversion Tracking

In affiliate marketing, conversions are the holy grail. Whether it's a sale, a lead generation form submission, or another desired action, conversions are the ultimate measure of success. Conversion tracking is the process of monitoring and recording these actions to understand how effectively your traffic is turning into valuable outcomes.

Here's why conversion tracking is essential:

1. Performance Evaluation: Conversion tracking allows you to evaluate the performance of your affiliate marketing campaigns accurately. It answers the pivotal question: Is your traffic translating into meaningful results? Without tracking, you're navigating blindly.

2. Optimization: Tracking conversions empowers you to optimize your strategies. By knowing what works and what doesn't, you can refine your content, ad campaigns, and audience targeting to improve conversion rates.

3. Return on Investment (ROI): Knowing which traffic sources and affiliate partnerships drive the most conversions helps you calculate ROI accurately. This data is vital for making informed decisions about where to allocate your resources.

4. Affiliate Partner Assessment: If you're working with multiple affiliate partners or programs, conversion tracking allows you to assess their performance objectively. You can determine which partners deliver the highest-quality traffic and conversions.

Tools and Methods for Conversion Tracking

Now, let's explore the tools and methods you can use for effective conversion tracking:

1. Google Analytics: Google Analytics is a powerful, free tool that provides in-depth insights into website traffic and conversions. It allows you to set up conversion goals and track e-commerce transactions if you're promoting products as an affiliate.

2. Affiliate Network Tracking: Many affiliate networks offer their own tracking tools and dashboards. These platforms provide valuable data on clicks, conversions, and earnings related to your affiliate partnerships.

3. UTM Parameters: Urchin Tracking Module (UTM) parameters are tags added to your URLs to track the performance of specific campaigns or sources. They're especially useful for tracking the effectiveness of different marketing channels or affiliate campaigns.

4. Conversion Pixels: Some affiliate programs provide conversion pixels or tracking codes that you can place on your website. These pixels record conversions and send the data back to the affiliate program's platform.

5. CRM and Email Marketing Platforms: If you're using email marketing for affiliate promotions, platforms like Mailchimp or HubSpot offer conversion tracking features. You can monitor how email campaigns drive conversions.

6. Heatmaps and Session Recording: Tools like Hotjar or Crazy Egg provide insights into user behavior on your website. While not conversion tracking tools per se, they can help you identify areas where visitors drop off before converting.

7. A/B Testing: Implement A/B testing to compare different versions of your affiliate landing pages or content. Track conversions on each version to determine which one performs better.

8. Affiliate Dashboard Metrics: Your affiliate program's dashboard should provide conversion tracking metrics, including click-through rates (CTR), conversion rates, and earnings per click (EPC).

In the treasure hunt of affiliate marketing, conversion tracking is your trusty map and compass. It guides you toward the treasures you seek – the conversions that define your success. By implementing the right tools and methods, you can not only measure your progress but also make data-driven decisions to enhance your affiliate marketing strategy and maximize your returns.

5.3.3 Traffic Sources Analysis: The Compass to Optimize Your Affiliate Marketing

Picture your affiliate marketing venture as a thriving garden, and your traffic sources as the various streams that nourish it. To ensure your garden flourishes, you need to understand the nature and quality of these streams. That's where traffic sources analysis comes in – it's your key to optimizing your affiliate marketing efforts. In this section, we'll dive into the significance of analyzing traffic sources and how this understanding can serve as your compass for optimization.

The Significance of Traffic Sources Analysis

In the digital realm, traffic doesn't arrive as a monolithic entity. It's a diverse ecosystem, with various sources contributing visitors to your affiliate platform. These sources can include search engines, social media, email marketing, paid advertising, referral links, and more. Understanding the origin of your traffic is crucial for several reasons:

1. Performance Evaluation: Different traffic sources have varying levels of effectiveness. Some sources may bring in high-converting, engaged visitors, while others might deliver low-quality traffic. By analyzing traffic sources, you can assess which channels are driving the most valuable visitors.

2. Resource Allocation: Your time, effort, and budget are limited resources. Knowing which traffic sources perform best allows you to allocate your resources more effectively. You can invest more in sources that yield results and adjust or eliminate those that don't.

3. Optimization: Traffic sources analysis provides insights into how to optimize your strategies. For example, if you discover that search engine traffic converts well, you can focus on improving your SEO efforts. If social media traffic is lacking, you can adjust your social media marketing strategy.

4. Goal Alignment: Different traffic sources may align better with specific goals. For instance, email marketing might excel at lead generation, while paid advertising could be ideal for driving sales. Aligning traffic sources with your goals ensures you're not just getting traffic but the right kind of traffic.

5. Partnerships and Affiliations: If you're working with affiliate partners or marketing platforms, analyzing traffic sources helps you assess their performance. You can identify which partners are delivering high-quality traffic and which ones need adjustments.

Understanding Traffic Sources

To analyze traffic sources effectively, consider the following aspects:

Source Type: Categorize traffic sources into groups like organic (from search engines), referral (from other websites), social (from social media platforms), direct (people who type your URL), and paid (from advertising campaigns).

Quality Metrics: Look at metrics like conversion rates, bounce rates, and session durations for each traffic source. High conversion rates and longer session durations indicate high-quality traffic.

Audience Behavior: Analyze how visitors from different sources behave on your site. Do they visit multiple pages, engage with your content, or make purchases?

Keyword Analysis: If you're getting organic search traffic, analyze the keywords that bring visitors to your site. Optimize your content for relevant keywords to attract more of your target audience.

Geographic Data: Determine where your traffic is coming from geographically. This insight can help you tailor your content or marketing efforts to specific regions.

Referral Sources: For referral traffic, identify which websites or platforms are sending visitors your way. Build relationships with high-performing referrers.

Tracking Tools: Use analytics tools like Google Analytics, affiliate program dashboards, and UTM parameters to track and attribute traffic accurately.

In the intricate web of affiliate marketing, traffic sources analysis is your compass, guiding you toward the fertile streams and away from the barren ones. It enables you to make informed decisions, optimize your strategies, and cultivate a thriving garden of affiliate success. By continually monitoring and adjusting your approach based on traffic source insights, you'll nurture a flourishing affiliate marketing venture.

5.3.4 Iterative Improvement: Navigating the Ever-Evolving Traffic Landscape

In the realm of affiliate marketing, success isn't a one-time achievement; it's a continuous journey. Think of it as a perpetual voyage through a dynamic and ever-evolving landscape. In this section, we'll explore the concept of iterative improvement in traffic generation and optimization. You'll discover why affiliate marketers must embrace an iterative approach and gain insights into strategies for ongoing enhancement based on data analysis.

The Essence of Iterative Improvement

Imagine you're sailing a ship through uncharted waters. You wouldn't set sail once and hope for the best; you'd constantly adjust your course based on changing winds, currents, and discoveries along the way. Similarly, in affiliate marketing, your journey to success is an ongoing process of refinement and adaptation.

Iterative improvement involves:

1. **Continuous Data Analysis:** Regularly analyzing traffic data to understand its trends and patterns. This process provides insights into what's working and what's not.
2. **Adjustments and Optimization:** Making informed adjustments to your strategies, content, and traffic sources based on the data. Optimization aims to enhance the effectiveness of your efforts.
3. **Testing and Experimentation:** Trying out new approaches, A/B testing different content or marketing methods, and experimenting with traffic sources to identify improvements.
4. **Goal Reassessment:** Revisiting your affiliate marketing goals and ensuring that your efforts align with those objectives. Goals may evolve as your venture progresses.

Strategies for Iterative Improvement

Here are strategies for implementing an iterative approach to traffic generation and optimization:

1. A/B Testing: Experiment with variations of your content or landing pages to determine which versions perform better. Test elements like headlines, images, call-to-action buttons, and layouts.

2. Content Refresh: Regularly update and refresh your evergreen content. Add new information, improve the visual appeal, and ensure that the content remains relevant and valuable.

3. Keyword Refinement: Continuously refine your keyword strategy based on search trends and performance data. Optimize existing content and create new content targeting high-performing keywords.

4. Performance Metrics Monitoring: Keep a close eye on performance metrics such as conversion rates, bounce rates, and session durations. If you notice declines, investigate and take corrective actions.

5. Traffic Source Diversification: Don't rely too heavily on a single traffic source. Diversify your traffic channels to reduce risk and increase stability.

6. Audience Feedback: Pay attention to feedback from your audience. Comments, emails, and social media interactions can provide valuable insights into their preferences and needs.

7. Stay Informed: Affiliate marketing is an ever-changing field. Stay updated on industry trends, algorithm changes, and emerging technologies that could impact your traffic strategies.

8. Collaborate and Network: Engage with fellow affiliate marketers, join forums or groups, and participate in discussions. Networking can provide fresh perspectives and opportunities for collaboration.

9. Goal Realignment: Periodically review your affiliate marketing goals. Are they still relevant? Are there new opportunities to pursue? Adjust your goals as needed to reflect your evolving aspirations.

10. Patience and Persistence: Understand that iterative improvement takes time and patience. Not every adjustment will yield immediate results, but consistent effort and learning will lead to long-term success.

Embracing an iterative approach in affiliate marketing is akin to mastering the art of navigation. You're not only steering your ship but also adapting to the ever-changing seascape. By continually analyzing, adjusting, and optimizing your traffic generation efforts, you'll not only survive but thrive in the dynamic world of affiliate marketing. Your journey is a testament to your adaptability and commitment to success.

CHAPTER 6: MONETIZATION MASTERY

Welcome to a comprehensive exploration of the art and science behind turning your affiliate traffic into a steady stream of earnings. In this section, we'll delve deep into the strategies and tactics that will help you craft click-worthy affiliate links, track your earnings with precision, and amplify your monetization efforts to their fullest potential. Whether you're a novice affiliate marketer or an experienced pro, the insights in this section will propel you toward mastery in the world of affiliate monetization.

6.1 The Monetization Puzzle

In the realm of affiliate marketing, the monetization puzzle holds the key to transforming your efforts into revenue. In this section, we'll delve into the intricacies of monetization, exploring the diverse revenue models and strategies to create compelling affiliate links. Get ready to unlock the full earning potential of your affiliate marketing endeavors.

6.1.1 Understanding Monetization in Affiliate Marketing: The Art of Earning

Monetization, in the captivating realm of affiliate marketing, is the process of turning your hard-earned traffic into tangible earnings. It's the alchemy that transforms clicks, views, and engagement into dollars and cents. In this section, we embark on a journey to grasp the essence of monetization in affiliate marketing, unveiling the magic that happens when you seamlessly connect your audience with valuable products or services.

The Essence of Monetization

At its core, monetization in affiliate marketing is the tangible reward for your efforts in driving traffic to a merchant's products or services. It's the symbiotic relationship where you, the affiliate marketer, act as the bridge between potential customers and the products they seek.

Here's how the magic unfolds:

1. **Traffic Generation:** As an affiliate marketer, you've honed your skills in attracting visitors to your platform, whether it's a blog, website, or social media channel. You've built trust, created engaging content, and established your authority in your niche. Your audience trusts your recommendations and values your insights.
2. **Affiliate Partnerships:** You've carefully selected affiliate programs that align with your niche and resonate with your audience. These programs provide you with unique affiliate links or promotional materials.
3. **Seamless Integration:** You seamlessly incorporate these affiliate links or promotional materials into your content, whether it's in blog posts, product reviews, videos, or social media posts. You're not just promoting products; you're providing value by addressing your audience's needs.
4. **Audience Engagement:** Your audience, driven by genuine interest and trust, clicks on your affiliate links and explores the products or services you recommend.

They might make purchases, sign up for services, or take other desired actions.

5. **Commission Earnings:** When your audience takes these actions through your affiliate links, you earn commissions. These earnings are your tangible rewards for the value you've brought to both your audience and the merchant.

Generating Affiliate Earnings from Traffic

Affiliate earnings originate from the traffic you've carefully nurtured and cultivated. Here's a breakdown of how this process works:

- **Click-Throughs:** When your audience clicks on your affiliate links, it signifies their interest and intent to explore further. Each click is a potential step towards earnings.
- **Conversion Actions:** Beyond clicks, conversions are the pivotal moments when your audience takes actions that benefit the merchant. These actions can vary, from making purchases to signing up for newsletters or filling out forms.
- **Commission Models:** Affiliate programs employ various commission models, such as Cost Per Sale (CPS), Cost Per Acquisition (CPA), or Cost Per Click (CPC). Depending on the model, you earn a portion of the sale value, a flat fee for each acquisition, or compensation for every click generated.
- **Tracking Mechanisms:** Affiliate tracking mechanisms and cookies play a vital role in attributing conversions to your efforts. They ensure that you receive credit for the actions your audience takes after clicking your affiliate links.

In essence, monetization in affiliate marketing is the tangible expression of the value you provide to your audience and the trust you've cultivated. It's the financial recognition of your ability to connect people with solutions to their needs and desires. As we dive deeper into this section, we'll explore the various facets of monetization, from crafting click-worthy affiliate links to tracking and amplifying your earnings, empowering you to master the art of earning through affiliate marketing.

6.1.2 Diverse Monetization Strategies: Beyond Affiliate Links

While affiliate links are a powerful avenue for earning in the world of affiliate marketing, they are just one piece of the monetization puzzle. In this section, we'll expand your horizons by introducing a range of diverse monetization strategies that can help you maximize your earnings potential. These strategies go beyond traditional affiliate links and open up new avenues for revenue generation.

1. Contextual Advertising:

Contextual advertising is a dynamic way to monetize your content by displaying ads that are directly relevant to your audience's interests and the content they're engaging with. Two popular platforms for contextual advertising are Google AdSense and Media.net. These programs analyze your content's context and display ads that align with the topics you cover, providing a seamless and unobtrusive way to earn through ad clicks and impressions.

2. Sponsored Content:

Sponsored content is a collaboration between you and a brand or company willing to pay for exposure on your platform. This monetization strategy involves creating content —such as articles, videos, or social media posts—that promotes the sponsor's products or services. Sponsored content should always be transparently labeled to maintain trust with your audience.

3. Premium Content or Memberships:

Consider offering premium content or memberships to your dedicated audience. This could involve providing exclusive articles, in-depth guides, access to webinars, or a private community forum in exchange for a subscription fee. Premium content can be a lucrative way to monetize your most engaged followers.

4. Digital Products and Courses:

If you have expertise in your niche, you can create and sell digital products or online courses. These can include e-books, video tutorials, templates, or even one-on-one coaching sessions. Digital products and courses not only generate revenue but also position you as an authority in your field.

5. Email Marketing:

Your email list is a valuable asset for monetization. You can promote affiliate products, your own digital products, or sponsored content directly to your subscribers. Email marketing allows for personalized communication and can lead to higher conversion rates compared to other channels.

6. Merchandise and E-commerce:

If you have a strong personal brand, consider selling merchandise related to your niche. This could include branded apparel, accessories, or even physical products that align with your content. Setting up an e-commerce store can diversify your income streams.

7. Consulting and Services:

As your authority and reach grow, you may find opportunities to offer consulting or freelance services related to your niche. Whether it's providing marketing advice, content writing, or design services, your expertise can translate into additional income.

8. Crowdfunding and Donations:

Platforms like Patreon, Ko-fi, or Buy Me a Coffee allow your audience to support you directly through donations or subscriptions. If your content resonates strongly with your followers, they may be willing to contribute financially to help sustain your work.

9. Sponsored Webinars and Workshops:

Collaborate with brands or organizations to host sponsored webinars or workshops for your audience. These live events can provide valuable information and generate revenue through sponsorship fees or ticket sales.

By diversifying your monetization strategies, you can create a resilient income stream that isn't solely reliant on affiliate commissions. Each strategy has its unique advantages, and the key is to select those that align with your content, audience, and niche. As you explore these avenues, remember to maintain transparency and prioritize your audience's trust and engagement, ensuring that your monetization efforts enhance, rather than detract from, the value you provide.

6.1.3 Balancing Monetization and User Experience: The Art of Harmony

In the affiliate marketing universe, where monetization is the ultimate goal, there's a delicate tightrope walk that every affiliate marketer must master: the balance between monetization and user experience. While the allure of earnings is strong, it should never come at the expense of your audience's trust and satisfaction. In this section, we'll explore the art of maintaining a positive user experience while optimizing your monetization efforts.

The User Experience Imperative

First and foremost, it's crucial to understand that user experience (UX) is the cornerstone of your affiliate marketing success. A seamless, enjoyable, and trustworthy experience keeps your audience engaged and coming back for more. It's the trust you build with your audience that ultimately leads to higher conversion rates and sustained affiliate earnings.

Tips for Balancing Monetization and UX:

1. **Ad Placement and Integration:** Carefully consider the placement and integration of ads on your platform to avoid disrupting user experience. Ensure that ads are seamlessly integrated into your content flow to maintain a clean and uncluttered interface.

2. **Transparency:** Build trust with your audience by maintaining transparency about your monetization strategies. Clearly label sponsored content, affiliate links, and ads to show authenticity and credibility, fostering a sense of honesty with your users.

3. **Relevance and Value:** Prioritize providing relevant and valuable content to your audience. Monetization efforts should enhance, rather than detract from, the overall user experience. Focus on delivering the information, solutions, or entertainment that your audience seeks.

4. **Mobile Optimization:** Optimize your website for mobile devices as more users access content through smartphones and tablets. A mobile-friendly site ensures a positive user experience, which can boost engagement and earnings.

5. **Page Load Speed:** Optimize your website's performance to maintain fast page load speeds. Slow-loading pages can deter users and negatively impact search engine rankings, affecting both user experience and monetization potential.

6. **User Feedback:** Actively seek and listen to user

feedback to gain insights into how monetization strategies affect their experience. Adjust your approach based on their input to ensure their needs are met.

7. **Content Quality:** Maintain a commitment to high-quality, informative, and engaging content. Quality content is your primary asset for attracting and retaining your audience, contributing to both user satisfaction and monetization success.

8. **Testing and Optimization:** Continuously test and optimize your website's layout, ad placements, and content formats. Utilize A/B testing to identify the most effective strategies for balancing monetization and user experience.

9. **Audience-Centric Approach:** Always prioritize your audience's needs and preferences. Ensure that your monetization strategies align with their interests and expectations, keeping their satisfaction at the forefront of your decisions.

Remember that long-term success in affiliate marketing hinges on the trust you build with your audience. While monetization is essential, it should be a natural extension of the value you provide. When done right, monetization enhances the user experience by offering relevant and valuable opportunities rather than disrupting it. Striking this balance is an ongoing journey that requires attention, adaptation, and a deep commitment to both your audience and your affiliate marketing goals.

6.2 Crafting Click-Worthy Affiliate Links

In the ever-evolving landscape of affiliate marketing, crafting click-worthy affiliate links is an art and science combined. These links are the conduits that connect your audience to products or services, and their effectiveness can significantly impact your earnings. In this section, we'll delve into the strategies and techniques that transform ordinary links into irresistible invitations for your audience to explore and purchase.

6.2.1 The Art of Affiliate Link Creation: Crafting Click-Worthy Connections

Affiliate links are the lifeblood of your affiliate marketing endeavors. They are the bridges that connect your audience to the products or services you promote, and their effectiveness can make all the difference in your affiliate earnings. In this section, we'll explore the art and science of affiliate link creation, shedding light on why well-crafted affiliate links matter and how you can create links that entice clicks.

The Significance of Well-Crafted Affiliate Links

Imagine your affiliate link as a digital salesperson. Its job is to convince your audience to take action, whether it's making a purchase, signing up for a service, or downloading an app. To fulfill this role effectively, affiliate links must be more than a mere URL; they should be persuasive invitations.

1. **Relevance:** The cornerstone of a click-worthy affiliate link is relevance. The product or service you're promoting must align seamlessly with your content and your audience's interests. If your link feels out of place or disconnected from your content, it's less likely to entice clicks.
2. **Clarity:** A clear and concise affiliate link is more likely to be clicked. Avoid lengthy, convoluted links that confuse your audience. Use URL shorteners to create clean, user-friendly links.
3. **Call to Action (CTA):** Every affiliate link should include a compelling call to action. Whether it's "Shop now," "Learn more," or "Get started," a well-crafted CTA tells your audience what to expect when they click the link.
4. **Trustworthiness:** Trust is a critical factor in affiliate

marketing. Make sure your audience knows that the link they're clicking is an affiliate link. Transparency builds trust and credibility.

5. **Testing:** Experiment with different link placements and styles to see what resonates most with your audience. A/B testing can provide valuable insights into which links are the most effective.

Creating Click-Worthy Affiliate Links

Creating enticing affiliate links requires attention to detail and a deep understanding of your audience. Here's a step-by-step guide to crafting click-worthy affiliate links:

Step 1: Choose the Right Product or Service: Select affiliate products or services that genuinely benefit your audience. Your enthusiasm and belief in the product will shine through in your promotional efforts.

Step 2: Generate Affiliate Links: Most affiliate programs provide tools to generate affiliate links. Use these resources to create your links, ensuring that they track referrals and commissions accurately.

Step 3: Incorporate the Link Naturally: Integrate your affiliate links organically into your content. They should fit seamlessly into the context of your articles, blog posts, or videos.

Step 4: Write Compelling Anchor Text: Instead of using generic text like "click here," use anchor text that communicates the value of clicking the link. For example, if you're promoting a fitness app, your anchor text could be "Achieve your fitness goals with this app."

Step 5: Add a Disclosure: Be transparent with your audience by including a disclosure that the link is an affiliate link. Honesty fosters trust.

Step 6: Test and Optimize: Monitor the performance of your affiliate links. Which ones are getting the most clicks and conversions? Use this data to refine your link strategy.

Remember, the goal is not just to generate clicks but to drive conversions. Crafting click-worthy affiliate links is about creating a seamless and persuasive path for your audience to follow, from initial interest to final action. When done skillfully, these links become valuable assets in your affiliate marketing arsenal, contributing to your success in the affiliate marketing landscape.

6.2.2 Incorporating Affiliate Links Naturally: The Art of Subtle Persuasion

In the realm of affiliate marketing, the art of seamlessly integrating affiliate links into your content is akin to weaving a compelling narrative—a narrative that captivates your audience while gently guiding them towards a desired action. In this section, we'll dive deep into the strategies and techniques that make the incorporation of affiliate links a natural and persuasive part of your content.

Why Natural Integration Matters

Imagine your affiliate links as part of a carefully orchestrated symphony. When they harmonize seamlessly with your content, they enhance the overall experience for your audience. But if they clash or disrupt the flow, they can create dissonance, potentially deterring clicks and conversions. Here's why natural integration matters:

1. **User Experience:** The paramount concern is user experience. If your content reads like a sales pitch, it may deter readers or viewers. Natural integration ensures that your audience engages with your content without feeling pressured or bombarded with promotional material.
2. **Credibility:** Your audience trusts you for your

expertise and unbiased recommendations. Natural integration preserves that trust by presenting affiliate products or services as valuable additions to the content, rather than the sole focus.

3. **Engagement:** Well-integrated affiliate links are more likely to be clicked because they enhance the user experience. When your audience sees these links as helpful resources or solutions, they're more inclined to explore them.

Effective Strategies for Natural Integration:

1. **Contextual Relevance:** Context is key. Place affiliate links where they naturally fit within your content. For example, if you're reviewing a fitness product, include affiliate links when discussing its features or benefits.

2. **Educational Approach:** Educate your audience about the products or services you're promoting. Provide in-depth information and explain how they can address specific needs or solve problems.

3. **Storytelling:** Incorporate affiliate products or services into your stories or narratives. Share personal experiences or case studies that demonstrate how these offerings have made a positive impact.

4. **Use of Visuals:** Visual content, such as images, infographics, or videos, provides excellent opportunities for affiliate link placement. Include links in image captions or video descriptions when they're relevant to the visual content.

5. **Comparison Guides:** Create comparison articles or videos where you evaluate multiple products or services in your niche. Include affiliate links for each option, allowing your audience to make informed choices.

6. **Resource Lists:** Compile resource lists or recommended tools related to your niche. Affiliate

links can naturally find a place here, offering your audience a convenient way to access these resources.

7. **Problem-Solution Approach:** Identify common problems or pain points within your niche and present affiliate products or services as solutions. Explain how they address these challenges effectively.

Example of Natural Integration:

Suppose you run a travel blog, and you're reviewing a popular backpack for backpackers. Instead of simply saying, "Click here to buy the backpack," you could incorporate it naturally like this:

"During my recent trek through the Himalayas, I relied on the [Backpack Name] to carry all my essentials. Its spacious compartments and ergonomic design made it a perfect companion for the journey. If you're planning your own adventure, you can check out the [Backpack Name] here."

In this example, the affiliate link seamlessly fits within the context of the review, offering value to the reader without interrupting the narrative flow.

Natural integration of affiliate links is an art that requires finesse and an in-depth understanding of your audience. When done effectively, it not only enhances your affiliate marketing efforts but also elevates the overall quality of your content. Remember, the goal is to empower your audience with valuable recommendations and solutions while earning commissions in the process.

6.2.3 Disclosing Affiliate Relationships: The Bedrock of Trust

In the dynamic world of affiliate marketing, maintaining trust with your audience is paramount. One of the foundational pillars of trust in this realm is transparent affiliate marketing practices. In this section, we'll delve into the significance of disclosing affiliate relationships and provide a comprehensive guide on when and how to do it effectively.

Why Transparency Matters

Transparency is not just a buzzword; it's the linchpin that holds your affiliate marketing strategy together. Here's why it matters:

1. **Trust Building:** Transparency is the key to building and preserving trust with your audience. When you openly disclose your affiliate relationships, you demonstrate honesty and integrity, which are qualities that resonate with your audience.
2. **Legal Compliance:** In many regions, including the United States, the Federal Trade Commission (FTC) mandates clear and conspicuous disclosure of affiliate relationships. Failing to comply with these regulations can lead to legal consequences.
3. **Credibility:** Transparent affiliate marketing enhances your credibility as a trusted source of information. Your audience is more likely to take your recommendations seriously when they know you have their best interests at heart.

When and How to Disclose Affiliate Relationships:

1. **Early and Clearly:** Disclose your affiliate relationship at the beginning of the content or as close to the affiliate link as possible. Make it clear to your audience that you may earn a commission if they make a purchase through your affiliate link.
2. **Use Clear Language:** Be explicit in your disclosure. Avoid vague or cryptic language. Use clear and straightforward terms that your audience can easily understand. For example, phrases like "This post contains affiliate links" or "I may earn a commission if you click and make a purchase" are effective.
3. **In Multiple Places:** Don't rely on a single disclosure; include it in multiple locations within your content. Mention it in the introduction, near affiliate links, and

in your website's footer or disclosure policy.

4. **Visual Cues:** Use visual cues like asterisks (*) or icons next to affiliate links to draw attention to them. However, these cues should be accompanied by clear text disclosures.

5. **Dedicated Disclosure Page:** Consider creating a dedicated "Disclosure" or "Affiliate Disclosure" page on your website. Link to this page from relevant sections of your content.

6. **Video and Audio:** If you produce video or audio content, verbally disclose your affiliate relationships at the beginning and mention it in the video or episode description.

7. **Social Media:** Extend transparency to your social media channels when sharing affiliate links. Use hashtags like #ad, #affiliate, or #sponsored to alert your followers to your affiliate relationships.

Example of Effective Disclosure:

Let's say you're promoting a skincare product on your blog. A transparent disclosure in your article could look like this:

"**Disclosure:** This post contains affiliate links, which means I may earn a commission if you click through and make a purchase. Rest assured, I only recommend products I genuinely believe in and have personally tested."

In this example, the disclosure is clear, placed at the beginning of the content, and reassures the audience of your commitment to honesty and product quality.

The Bottom Line:

Transparency is not just a legal requirement; it's a fundamental principle that underpins ethical affiliate marketing. By disclosing your affiliate relationships openly and honestly, you foster trust, credibility, and lasting relationships with your audience. Remember, your audience's trust is a valuable asset in the affiliate marketing world, and it's worth nurturing through transparent practices.

6.3 Tracking and Amplifying Earnings

In the world of affiliate marketing, success isn't solely about promoting products or services; it's also about understanding and optimizing the financial aspect of your endeavors. Tracking and amplifying earnings are essential components of this journey. In this section, we'll explore the strategies and tools that empower affiliate marketers to monitor their earnings, make informed decisions, and ultimately, boost their income streams.

6.3.1 Affiliate Earnings Tracking Tools: Your Path to Informed Decisions

As an affiliate marketer, your journey to success is intrinsically tied to your ability to monitor and optimize your earnings. In this section, we'll unveil the power of affiliate earnings tracking tools and how they can be your trusted companions in this dynamic landscape.

The Crucial Role of Tracking

Tracking your affiliate earnings isn't merely an optional task; it's the compass that guides your decisions. Here's why it's essential:

1. **Performance Assessment:** Tracking allows you to assess the performance of your affiliate campaigns and initiatives. It provides real-time insights into what's working and what isn't, enabling you to make data-driven adjustments.
2. **Optimization:** Armed with accurate data, you can optimize your strategies. Whether it's refining your content, adjusting your promotional methods, or identifying high-converting products, tracking

empowers you to fine-tune your approach.

3. **Revenue Maximization:** Tracking helps you identify high-earning channels, products, or campaigns. By capitalizing on these top performers, you can maximize your revenue potential.

Affiliate Earnings Tracking Tools

Now, let's explore the array of tools and platforms designed to make affiliate earnings tracking a seamless and efficient process:

1. **Affiliate Networks:** Most affiliate networks offer robust tracking dashboards. They provide real-time data on clicks, conversions, commissions, and more. Some popular affiliate networks include Amazon Associates, ShareASale, and CJ Affiliate.
2. **Google Analytics:** This free, versatile tool offers valuable insights into your website's performance. It can track affiliate links, monitor traffic sources, and measure conversion rates.
3. **Affiliate Tracking Software:** There are dedicated affiliate tracking software solutions available, such as Voluum, Post Affiliate Pro, and ClickMeter. These tools offer advanced tracking capabilities, including granular performance analysis and A/B testing.
4. **Custom Tracking Solutions:** Some affiliate marketers opt for custom tracking solutions, especially if they have specific tracking requirements. These solutions may involve using UTM parameters or hiring developers to create tailored tracking systems.

Benefits of Real-Time Monitoring

Real-time monitoring of affiliate earnings brings a host of advantages to your affiliate marketing efforts:

1. **Timely Adjustments:** With real-time data, you can make immediate adjustments to underperforming

campaigns or capitalize on sudden surges in traffic.

2. **Fraud Prevention:** Real-time tracking allows you to detect and address potential fraud or click discrepancies promptly.
3. **Instant Gratification:** Watching commissions roll in real-time can be motivating and satisfying, spurring you to work even harder.
4. **Flexible Decision-Making:** Real-time data empowers you to make agile decisions. Whether it's increasing ad spend on a successful campaign or pausing a non-converting one, you're in control.

Conclusion

In the fast-paced world of affiliate marketing, tracking your earnings isn't just a best practice; it's a necessity. These tracking tools, combined with the benefits of real-time monitoring, form the bedrock of your ability to make informed decisions, optimize your strategies, and ultimately amplify your earnings. As you navigate this landscape, remember that the insights gleaned from tracking are the keys to unlocking your affiliate marketing success.

6.3.2 Analyzing Earnings Data: Transforming Numbers into Insights

Earnings data in affiliate marketing is like a treasure trove waiting to be discovered. It's not just about the numbers; it's about understanding what those numbers reveal and how you can use them to propel your affiliate marketing journey. In this section, we'll delve into the art of interpreting earnings data, identifying trends, and drawing actionable insights that can elevate your affiliate game.

The Power of Earnings Analysis

Earnings data isn't just a report card of your efforts; it's a roadmap to optimization and growth. Here's why analyzing earnings data is crucial:

1. **Strategic Decision-Making:** Earnings data empowers you to make informed decisions. By dissecting the numbers, you can pinpoint what's working and what needs improvement.
2. **Identifying Trends:** Trends are the hidden gems within earnings data. They reveal patterns, seasonality, and shifts in consumer behavior, allowing you to capitalize on opportunities.
3. **Optimizing Campaigns:** Armed with insights, you can optimize your affiliate campaigns. Whether it's tweaking your content strategy, adjusting ad spend, or diversifying your product offerings, earnings analysis guides your actions.

Interpreting Earnings Data:

Here's a step-by-step guide on how to effectively interpret earnings data and draw actionable insights:

1. **Segmentation:** Begin by segmenting your earnings data. Break it down by various factors, such as products, campaigns, traffic sources, or time periods. This segmentation allows for a more granular analysis.

2. **Identify High Performers:** Look for top-performing products, campaigns, or channels. What sets them apart? Is there a common element contributing to their success? For instance, do certain product categories consistently generate higher commissions?

3. **Spot Trends:** Analyze earnings data over time. Are there seasonal trends or consistent growth patterns? For example, do earnings typically spike during holiday seasons or special promotions?

4. **Conversion Funnel Analysis:** Trace the customer journey from the initial click to the final purchase. Identify drop-off

points and bottlenecks in the conversion process. Are there specific pages or steps that need optimization?

5. **Traffic Quality:** Evaluate the quality of your traffic sources. Are certain sources driving more high-converting clicks than others? If so, consider reallocating your efforts and budget towards these sources.

6. **Cost vs. Earnings:** Calculate the return on investment (ROI) for your campaigns. Are you spending more on advertising than you're earning in commissions? Adjust your budget or focus on higher ROI campaigns.

Example of Actionable Insights:

Let's say you've been promoting a range of tech products, and your earnings analysis reveals that gaming laptops consistently generate the highest commissions. This insight can lead to several actions:

- **Content Focus:** Shift your content strategy to create more in-depth reviews and guides on gaming laptops.
- **Keyword Optimization:** Optimize your content for gaming laptop-related keywords to improve search engine rankings.
- **Paid Advertising:** Allocate a larger portion of your budget to campaigns promoting gaming laptops.

Earnings data isn't just a report; it's a blueprint for success in affiliate marketing. By dissecting the numbers, identifying trends, and drawing actionable insights, you can fine-tune your strategies, capitalize on opportunities, and continuously optimize your affiliate marketing efforts. In this data-driven landscape, your ability to transform numbers into actions is the key to unlocking your full affiliate potential.

6.3.3 Strategies for Earnings Growth: Elevating Your Affiliate Game

In the dynamic world of affiliate marketing, the pursuit of increased earnings is a perpetual quest. To succeed, affiliate marketers must not only monitor and analyze their earnings but also implement strategies that drive consistent growth. In this section, we'll explore a spectrum of strategies designed to optimize your affiliate marketing efforts and elevate your earnings to new heights.

1. Split Testing for Perfection:

Split testing, or A/B testing, is a fundamental strategy for refining your affiliate campaigns. It involves creating multiple versions of a webpage, ad, or email, each with slight variations. By comparing their performance, you can determine what resonates best with your audience.

For example, you could split test different ad headlines, calls to action, or even entire landing pages. Over time, this iterative approach helps you fine-tune your content for higher conversions, which directly translates to increased earnings.

2. Diversify Your Offerings:

While it's essential to focus on your niche, diversifying your product or service offerings can open new revenue streams. Explore complementary products or services that align with your niche. By expanding your portfolio, you not only cater to a broader audience but also reduce the reliance on a single product.

Diversification also extends to traffic sources. Relying solely on one traffic channel can be risky. Branch out to multiple channels like SEO, social media, email marketing, and paid advertising to create a more resilient affiliate marketing ecosystem.

3. Audience Engagement and Retention:

Engaging your audience isn't just about attracting new visitors; it's also about retaining and nurturing your existing ones. Engaged audiences are more likely to trust your recommendations and make repeat purchases, boosting your earnings over time.

- **Email Marketing:** Build and nurture an email subscriber list. Use it to deliver valuable content, promotions, and affiliate recommendations to a receptive audience.
- **Content Quality:** Continuously improve the quality of your content. Address your audience's pain points, answer their questions, and provide actionable insights.
- **Community Building:** Foster a sense of community among your audience. Engage with them through comments, social media, and forums to build trust and loyalty.

4. **Advanced Keyword Strategies:**

If you're leveraging SEO as a traffic source, advanced keyword strategies can significantly impact your earnings. Beyond basic keyword research, explore:

- **Long-Tail Keywords:** Target longer and more specific keywords that often have lower competition but higher conversion rates.
- **Keyword Trends:** Stay updated on keyword trends in your niche. Create content around trending topics to capture seasonal or emerging opportunities.
- **Competitor Analysis:** Analyze the keywords your competitors are targeting and identify gaps or untapped keyword opportunities.

5. **Continual Learning and Adaptation:**

The affiliate marketing landscape is ever-evolving. To sustain and increase your earnings, commit to continuous learning and adaptation. Stay updated on industry trends, algorithm changes, and new tools.

Participate in affiliate marketing forums, attend webinars, and read industry publications. The more you invest in staying informed, the better equipped you'll be to adapt and thrive.

Earnings growth in affiliate marketing is not a one-time achievement; it's a journey of consistent improvement and optimization. By employing strategies like split testing, diversification, audience engagement, advanced keyword tactics, and a commitment to learning, you can not only boost your earnings but also build a sustainable and thriving affiliate marketing business. Remember, in this landscape, the path to higher earnings is paved with innovation, adaptability, and a deep understanding of your audience and niche.

6.3.4 Scaling Your Monetization Efforts: Expanding Your Affiliate Empire

Scaling your affiliate marketing efforts is like turning a small garden into a thriving forest. It's about leveraging your existing successes to reach broader audiences, tap into new niches, and ultimately boost your earnings. In this section, we'll explore the exciting world of scaling and how it can be your ticket to substantial affiliate income.

1. Leveraging Your Best-Performing Assets:

One of the most effective ways to scale your affiliate marketing is by identifying your best-performing assets and replicating their success. These assets could be high-converting content, successful advertising campaigns, or top-performing products. For instance, if you've created a product review video that generates substantial affiliate income, consider producing similar videos for other products in your niche. By applying the same formula, you can scale your content creation efforts while maintaining a proven strategy.

2. Expanding Across Niche Verticals:

While focusing on a niche is essential, it doesn't mean you're limited to just one. Once you've established a strong presence in your primary niche, consider expanding into related verticals. For example, if your niche is fitness equipment, you could explore supplements, workout apparel, or fitness apps.

This diversification not only increases your potential audience but also minimizes risk. A downturn in one niche can be offset by growth in another, ensuring your earnings remain stable.

3. Collaborations and Partnerships:

Collaborating with other affiliates or complementary businesses can be a powerful scaling strategy. Joint ventures allow you to tap into each other's audiences and expertise, amplifying your reach.

Consider partnerships like co-hosted webinars, joint giveaways, or content collaborations. These initiatives introduce your affiliate products to a new, engaged audience, resulting in increased earnings for both parties.

4. Automation and Delegation:

As your affiliate empire expands, managing every aspect of your business on your own becomes challenging. Invest in automation tools that can handle tasks like email marketing, social media scheduling, and data analysis.

Moreover, consider delegating certain tasks to virtual assistants or freelancers. This frees up your time to focus on high-impact activities like strategy development and content creation.

5. Scalable Paid Advertising Campaigns:

If paid advertising is part of your affiliate strategy, scaling requires careful planning. Begin with a well-performing campaign and gradually increase your ad spend as you see positive returns.

Segment your audience to create highly targeted campaigns. Continuously optimize your ad creatives, ad copy, and targeting options to maximize ROI.

6. Data-Driven Decision-Making:

Scaling should be data-driven. Regularly review your earnings data to identify scaling opportunities. Are certain products consistently generating high commissions? Are there untapped traffic sources with potential?

By analyzing your data, you can make informed decisions on where and how to scale effectively.

Scaling your affiliate marketing efforts is the path to substantially boosting your earnings. By leveraging your best-performing assets, expanding across niche verticals, seeking collaborations, automating tasks, and making data-driven decisions, you can create a thriving affiliate empire. Remember that scaling isn't about growing for the sake of growth; it's about maintaining profitability while reaching new heights. With careful planning and strategic execution, your affiliate income potential knows no bounds.

CHAPTER 7: BUILDING YOUR AFFILIATE EMPIRE

In the realm of affiliate marketing, success often comes to those who build not just businesses but empires. The journey from novice affiliate marketer to industry authority is marked by deliberate strategies, consistent effort, and the ability to overcome challenges. In this section, we'll delve into the blueprint for constructing your affiliate empire, strategies for scaling your affiliate endeavors, and methods for triumphing over the obstacles that may come your way.

7.1 Blueprint for Success

In affiliate marketing, success doesn't happen by chance; it's meticulously crafted through a well-thought-out blueprint. This blueprint serves as the foundation for building a thriving affiliate business, providing a clear roadmap to follow. In this section, we'll unveil the essential elements of this blueprint, offering insights, strategies, and practical advice to help you navigate your path to affiliate marketing success.

7.1.1 The Affiliate Marketing Roadmap: Your Blueprint for Success

Navigating the world of affiliate marketing can often feel like embarking on a journey without a map. That's why having a well-defined roadmap is not just helpful—it's essential for your success. In this section, we'll introduce you to a step-by-step blueprint for affiliate marketing that will serve as your guiding light on this exciting adventure.

Step 1: Define Your Goals and Objectives

Every successful journey begins with a clear destination in mind. Start by setting specific and achievable goals for your affiliate marketing venture. Whether it's earning a certain income, building a loyal audience, or establishing authority in your niche, having defined objectives will keep you focused and motivated.

Step 2: Choose Your Niche Wisely

Your niche is the compass that directs your efforts. Take the time to research and select a niche that aligns with your interests, has market demand, and offers potential for growth. A well-chosen niche is the cornerstone of your success.

Step 3: Research and Select Affiliate Programs

With your niche in mind, scout for reputable affiliate programs that resonate with your audience. Look for programs that offer products or services relevant to your niche and have competitive commission structures. It's essential to partner with merchants who align with your values and goals.

Step 4: Craft Compelling Content

Content is the vehicle that carries your affiliate marketing message to your audience. Develop a content strategy that includes blog posts, videos, social media posts, and more. Your content should provide value, solve problems, and build trust with your audience.

Step 5: Drive Targeted Traffic

Once you have valuable content in place, it's time to attract your ideal audience. Utilize various traffic generation strategies, such as SEO, social media marketing, email campaigns, and paid advertising. Remember that the quality of your traffic is just as important as the quantity.

Step 6: Monetize Effectively
Maximize your affiliate earnings by strategically placing affiliate links within your content. Ensure that your monetization methods enhance rather than disrupt the user experience. Experiment with different approaches and analyze the results to optimize your strategies.

Step 7: Build and Nurture Relationships
Affiliate marketing isn't just about transactions; it's about building lasting relationships. Engage with your audience through comments, social media, and email. Foster trust and credibility to keep your audience coming back for more.

Step 8: Analyze, Adjust, and Scale
Regularly monitor your performance by analyzing data and key metrics. Identify what's working and what needs improvement. Adjust your strategies accordingly and scale up your successful campaigns. Affiliate marketing is a dynamic field, and continuous adaptation is key.

Step 9: Stay Informed and Evolve
The digital landscape and affiliate marketing industry are ever-changing. Stay informed about industry trends, emerging technologies, and evolving consumer behaviors. Continuously educate yourself and be open to adapting your approach to stay relevant.

Your Affiliate Marketing Odyssey

Consider this roadmap as your compass, guiding you through the twists and turns of affiliate marketing. While the journey may have challenges and detours, a well-structured approach based on these steps will increase your chances of success. Remember, affiliate marketing is a journey, not a destination, so enjoy the ride as you build your affiliate empire.

7.1.2 Setting Clear Goals: The North Star of Affiliate Marketing Success

In the vast landscape of affiliate marketing, setting clear and well-defined goals is akin to charting your course using the North Star—it provides direction and purpose to your journey. Without a doubt, goal setting is one of the foundational pillars of a successful affiliate marketing strategy. In this section, we'll delve into the significance of setting specific and achievable affiliate marketing goals and offer valuable tips for defining both short-term and long-term objectives.

The Significance of Setting Goals

Imagine embarking on a road trip without a destination in mind. You might drive aimlessly, making random turns, but you'll likely end up feeling lost and unfulfilled. Similarly, in affiliate marketing, having specific goals serves as your digital roadmap. Here's why goal setting matters:

1. **Clarity and Focus**: Goals bring clarity to your affiliate marketing efforts. They provide a clear picture of what you aim to achieve, helping you stay focused and avoid distractions. When your goals are well-defined, you know precisely where to direct your energy and resources.

2. **Motivation and Accountability**: Goals are powerful motivators. They give you a reason to work diligently, especially when faced with challenges. Additionally, setting goals holds you accountable for your progress. You can measure your performance against these objectives and adjust your strategies accordingly.

3. **Measurable Progress**: Goals are inherently measurable. This means you can track your progress, assess your achievements, and identify areas that need improvement. The ability to measure your success allows for data-driven decision-making.

Tips for Setting Specific Affiliate Marketing Goals

Now that you understand the importance of goals, let's explore some tips for setting specific and achievable affiliate marketing objectives:

1. **Be Specific**: Vague goals lead to vague results. Instead of setting a goal like "I want to make money," specify the exact amount you aim to earn within a specific timeframe. For example, "I want to earn $1,000 in affiliate commissions within the next three months."
2. **Break Down Long-Term Goals**: If you have long-term aspirations, break them down into smaller, short-term goals. This makes the larger objective more manageable and allows you to track progress more effectively.
3. **Make Them Achievable**: While ambition is admirable, ensure your goals are realistic and attainable. Setting goals that are too lofty can be demotivating if they're consistently out of reach. Start with smaller, achievable milestones and progressively aim higher as you gain experience.
4. **Include a Timeframe**: Every goal should have a timeframe attached to it. This creates a sense of urgency and helps you stay on track. For example, "I want to increase my website traffic by 20% in the next two months."
5. **Prioritize and Focus**: Avoid overwhelming yourself with too many goals simultaneously. Prioritize your objectives based on their importance and relevance to your affiliate marketing strategy. Concentrate your efforts on achieving one or two key goals at a time.
6. **Review and Adjust**: Goals are not set in stone. Regularly review your goals, assess your progress, and be open to adjusting them as needed. Sometimes, you may need to recalibrate your goals based on changing

circumstances or insights gained through analytics.

In affiliate marketing, setting clear and achievable goals is not just a best practice; it's your compass in the digital wilderness. With well-defined objectives, you'll have the direction, motivation, and tools needed to steer your affiliate marketing endeavors towards success. Whether you're aiming to increase your earnings, grow your audience, or establish authority in your niche, setting and pursuing your goals will guide you on your affiliate marketing odyssey.

7.1.3 Developing a Content Calendar: Your Roadmap to Affiliate Marketing Success

In the world of affiliate marketing, organization and strategic planning are key to achieving long-term success. One powerful tool that affiliate marketers often employ is a content calendar. A content calendar serves as your roadmap, helping you stay on track, maintain consistency, and maximize the impact of your affiliate marketing efforts. In this section, we'll delve into the benefits of creating a content calendar and provide valuable guidance on how to plan and schedule your affiliate content effectively.

The Benefits of a Content Calendar

Imagine setting out on a cross-country road trip without a map or GPS. You might end up lost, miss important landmarks, or waste valuable time backtracking. Similarly, in affiliate marketing, a content calendar is your digital map—a visual representation of your affiliate marketing journey. Here's why it's indispensable:

1. **Consistency**: Consistency is crucial in building trust and engagement with your audience. A content calendar ensures that you consistently deliver fresh, valuable content to your readers or viewers, keeping them engaged and returning for more.

2. **Strategic Planning**: With a content calendar, you can plan your content strategically. You can align your content with seasonal trends, product launches, or promotional campaigns, maximizing your affiliate marketing opportunities.

3. **Efficient Workflow**: It helps you manage your time and resources efficiently. By scheduling content in advance, you avoid last-minute rushes and ensure that you have ample time for research, creation, and promotion.

4. **Goal Alignment**: Your content calendar allows you to align your content with your affiliate marketing goals. Whether you aim to boost product sales, grow your email list, or increase website traffic, you can tailor your content to meet these objectives.

Creating Your Content Calendar: A Step-by-Step Guide

Now that you understand the advantages of a content calendar, let's explore how to create one effectively:

1. **Set Clear Objectives**: Begin by defining your affiliate marketing goals. What do you aim to achieve with your content? Are you focusing on product reviews, informative blog posts, or how-to videos? Your objectives will drive your content strategy.

2. **Identify Your Audience**: Understand your target audience's needs, preferences, and pain points. Knowing your audience helps you create content that resonates with them.

3. **Brainstorm Content Ideas**: Generate a list of content ideas relevant to your niche and audience. Consider seasonal topics, trending themes, and evergreen content that can provide long-term value.

4. **Prioritize Content**: Not all content is equal. Prioritize your ideas based on their alignment with your goals and your audience's interests. Decide which content is

essential and which can be supplementary.

5. **Set a Publishing Schedule**: Determine how frequently you'll publish content. Weekly, bi-weekly, or monthly schedules are common. Be realistic about your capacity to create high-quality content consistently.

6. **Plan Ahead**: Create a calendar for at least several months in advance. This allows you to plan content around important events and promotions.

7. **Allocate Resources**: Identify the resources you'll need for each piece of content, such as research, writing, graphics, and promotion. Ensure you have the necessary resources available when needed.

8. **Review and Adapt**: Regularly review your content calendar to assess its effectiveness. Adjust it based on audience feedback, performance metrics, and evolving affiliate marketing goals.

Tools like digital calendars, project management software, or even a simple spreadsheet can help you create and manage your content calendar effectively.

By developing a content calendar tailored to your affiliate marketing objectives, you'll not only streamline your workflow but also increase your chances of achieving your goals. It's your blueprint for success, guiding you through the affiliate marketing landscape with purpose and precision.

7.2 Scaling Your Affiliate Endeavors

In the journey of affiliate marketing, success often sparks a desire for growth and expansion. Scaling your affiliate endeavors involves taking the strategies and experiences that have brought you success and multiplying their impact. This chapter will delve into the art of scaling your affiliate marketing business, exploring strategies, challenges, and the path to triumph in the world of affiliate marketing at scale.

7.2.1 The Path to Scaling: Elevating Your Affiliate Marketing

Game

Scaling your affiliate marketing endeavors is like taking your thriving small business and expanding it into a well-established enterprise. It's a significant step that holds the promise of increased income, expanded reach, and the potential to turn your affiliate marketing venture into a sustainable source of revenue. In this section, we'll explore the compelling reasons and benefits behind scaling your affiliate marketing efforts.

The Reasons Behind Scaling

1. **Maximizing Earnings**: At its core, scaling is about maximizing your income potential. As you grow your affiliate marketing business, you can tap into a wider audience and promote more products or services, ultimately increasing your commission earnings.
2. **Diversification**: Scaling allows you to diversify your affiliate partnerships and income streams. Instead of relying on a single niche or affiliate program, you can explore multiple niches and work with various affiliate partners, reducing dependency on a single source.
3. **Economies of Scale**: As your affiliate marketing business grows, you can leverage economies of scale. This means that the more you produce (in this case, content or promotional materials), the lower the cost per unit. It can lead to increased efficiency and profitability.
4. **Enhanced Credibility**: Scaling often goes hand-in-hand with building a brand and online presence. A well-established brand can enhance your credibility as an affiliate marketer, making it easier to collaborate with reputable merchants and attract a loyal audience.
5. **Increased Impact**: Scaling allows you to reach a broader audience and have a more significant impact within your niche or niches. You can become a recognized authority in your field, which can translate

into more affiliate sales and commissions.

The Benefits of Scaling

1. **Higher Income Potential**: The most apparent benefit of scaling is the potential for higher income. With more content, more traffic, and more affiliate partnerships, your earnings can grow exponentially.
2. **Diversification**: Scaling enables you to diversify your income sources, reducing the risk associated with relying on a single niche or affiliate program. This diversification can provide stability and resilience in the face of market fluctuations.
3. **Efficiency**: As your affiliate marketing business expands, you'll likely become more efficient in content creation, promotion, and audience engagement. Streamlined processes and automation can save you time and effort.
4. **Leverage**: Scaling allows you to leverage your existing assets, such as a well-established website, email list, or social media following, to reach a larger audience and generate more conversions.
5. **Long-Term Sustainability**: A scaled affiliate marketing business can be more sustainable in the long run. It can provide a consistent source of passive income, giving you financial security and flexibility.

However, scaling isn't without its challenges and considerations. It requires careful planning, resource allocation, and a deep understanding of your niche and audience. In the following sections, we'll explore strategies for scaling your affiliate marketing business, triumphing over challenges, and achieving long-term success in the world of affiliate marketing at scale.

7.2.2 Outsourcing and Delegating: Expanding Your Affiliate Empire Efficiently

Scaling your affiliate marketing business often involves wearing many hats, from content creator to marketer to data analyst. As your venture grows, managing all aspects of it can become overwhelming and may limit your ability to reach your full potential. This is where the strategic use of outsourcing and delegating comes into play, allowing you to expand your affiliate empire efficiently and effectively.

Understanding Outsourcing and Delegating

Outsourcing and delegating involve entrusting certain tasks or responsibilities to others, either individuals or agencies, to help you manage your affiliate marketing operations. While you may have been a one-person show in the early stages of your affiliate journey, as you scale, you'll find that sharing the workload can be a game-changer.

Tasks to Consider Outsourcing

1. **Content Creation**: Content is the backbone of affiliate marketing. Outsourcing content creation to experienced writers can ensure a consistent flow of high-quality articles, blog posts, or product reviews.
2. **SEO and Keyword Research**: Search engine optimization (SEO) is vital for driving organic traffic. SEO experts can optimize your content and improve your website's visibility in search engine results.
3. **Graphic Design**: Visual content, including images and infographics, plays a crucial role in engaging your audience. Graphic designers can create eye-catching visuals that enhance your affiliate content.
4. **Email Marketing**: Managing an email list and running email marketing campaigns can be time-consuming. Outsourcing email marketing tasks can help you nurture and grow your subscriber base.
5. **Social Media Management**: Social media platforms are valuable for promoting your affiliate content.

Social media managers can handle posting schedules, engagement with followers, and the overall social media strategy.

6. **Paid Advertising**: If you're using paid advertising channels like Google Ads or Facebook Ads, consider working with experts who can optimize your ad campaigns for better ROI.

Benefits of Outsourcing and Delegating

1. **Focus on Core Competencies**: By outsourcing non-core tasks, you can focus on what you do best—creating content, building relationships with affiliate partners, and strategizing for growth.
2. **Efficiency**: Professionals or agencies specializing in specific tasks can often complete them more efficiently and with better results than you could on your own.
3. **Scalability**: Outsourcing allows you to scale without hiring full-time employees. You can adjust the level of support as needed, making it a flexible solution.
4. **Time Savings**: Delegating tasks frees up your time to work on high-impact activities that directly contribute to your affiliate marketing success.
5. **Expertise**: You gain access to the expertise of professionals in their respective fields, improving the quality of work in those areas.

Challenges and Considerations

While outsourcing and delegating offer numerous benefits, they come with their own set of challenges and considerations:

1. **Cost**: Hiring professionals or agencies may involve expenses. It's crucial to weigh the cost against the potential return on investment.
2. **Communication**: Effective communication is essential when working with outsourced teams or individuals. Clear expectations and regular updates are key to

success.

3. **Quality Control**: Maintaining quality standards is vital. You'll need processes in place to review and approve outsourced work.
4. **Security**: When sharing sensitive information or granting access to your affiliate accounts, ensure security measures are in place to protect your data.
5. **Management**: Managing multiple outsourced tasks can become complex. Consider using project management tools to stay organized.

Outsourcing and delegating can be a powerful strategy for scaling your affiliate marketing business. It allows you to tap into expertise, save time, and focus on strategic growth. By carefully selecting the tasks to outsource and managing your outsourced relationships effectively, you can expand your affiliate empire efficiently and reach new levels of success.

7.2.3 Leveraging Automation: Streamlining Your Affiliate Empire

Scaling your affiliate marketing endeavors isn't just about expanding your efforts; it's also about working smarter, not harder. One of the most effective ways to achieve this is by leveraging automation. Automation tools can streamline various aspects of your affiliate marketing processes, saving you time, improving efficiency, and ultimately helping you reach new heights in your affiliate empire.

The Power of Affiliate Marketing Automation

Affiliate marketing involves a multitude of tasks, from content creation to tracking conversions and managing affiliate relationships. While these tasks are essential, they can become overwhelming as your affiliate empire grows. Automation steps in to simplify and optimize these processes.

Here are some areas where automation can make a significant

impact:

1. **Email Marketing**: Email automation tools like Mailchimp or ConvertKit allow you to set up automated email sequences. You can nurture leads, send out newsletters, and promote affiliate products without manual intervention.
2. **Content Distribution**: Tools like Buffer and Hootsuite enable you to schedule and automate your social media posts. This ensures consistent promotion of your affiliate content across various platforms.
3. **Analytics and Reporting**: Tools like Google Analytics and affiliate tracking software provide automated data collection and reporting. You can easily monitor traffic, conversions, and earnings without manual record-keeping.
4. **Affiliate Link Management**: Affiliate link management tools help you organize and track your affiliate links. Some even provide insights into link performance and click-through rates.
5. **SEO Optimization**: SEO tools like Yoast SEO or SEMrush can automate the optimization of your content for search engines. They provide recommendations and analyze your content's SEO-friendliness.
6. **Conversion Tracking**: Conversion tracking tools automatically monitor and record affiliate conversions. This data is crucial for assessing the performance of affiliate programs and campaigns.

Recommended Affiliate Marketing Automation Tools

1. **Autoresponder Tools**: Consider using email marketing automation platforms like Mailchimp, ConvertKit, or AWeber for building and nurturing your email list.
2. **Social Media Schedulers**: Tools like Buffer, Hootsuite, or Later can help automate your social media posting

and content promotion.

3. **Analytics and Tracking**: Google Analytics, along with affiliate tracking software provided by affiliate programs, is essential for automated performance monitoring.
4. **Content Management Systems (CMS)**: CMS platforms like WordPress offer plugins and features for content scheduling and SEO optimization.
5. **Link Management**: Consider link management tools like ThirstyAffiliates or Pretty Links for organizing and tracking your affiliate links.

Automation Workflow Recommendations

1. **Email Sequences**: Set up automated email sequences to welcome new subscribers, provide value, and promote affiliate products gradually.
2. **Social Media Scheduling**: Create a content calendar and use scheduling tools to automate social media posts for consistent promotion.
3. **Scheduled Content**: Plan and schedule your content in advance using your CMS to maintain a consistent publishing schedule.
4. **SEO Optimization**: Use SEO plugins and tools to automate on-page SEO optimization for your articles and blog posts.
5. **Affiliate Link Organization**: Utilize link management tools to categorize and track your affiliate links efficiently.
6. **Conversion Tracking Alerts**: Set up alerts or notifications for significant affiliate conversions or milestones.
7. **Performance Reports**: Automate the generation of performance reports from your analytics and tracking tools to keep a close eye on your progress.

While automation can significantly enhance your affiliate

marketing efforts, it's essential to strike a balance. Some tasks, such as content creation and relationship building, require a personal touch. Evaluate your workflow and identify areas where automation can be most beneficial, allowing you to focus on strategic activities that require your unique expertise. By harnessing the power of automation, you can efficiently manage and scale your affiliate empire while achieving consistent results.

7.3 Triumphing Over Challenges

In the world of affiliate marketing, success often comes hand in hand with overcoming challenges and obstacles. As you've journeyed through this guide, you've learned the intricacies of affiliate marketing, niche selection, content creation, and monetization. Now, it's time to equip yourself with the knowledge and strategies needed to conquer the inevitable hurdles and triumph over the challenges that may arise along your affiliate marketing path. This chapter is your guide to resilience, problem-solving, and ultimately, triumph in the face of adversity.

7.3.1 Common Affiliate Marketing Challenges: Overcoming Obstacles for Success

As you embark on your affiliate marketing journey, it's essential to be aware of the challenges that lie ahead. Affiliate marketing, while rewarding, is not without its share of hurdles and obstacles. However, armed with knowledge and a proactive approach, you can navigate these challenges and emerge as a triumphant affiliate marketer. In this section, we'll identify and describe some common challenges faced by affiliate marketers, and we'll explore real-world examples that illustrate how these challenges can be overcome.

1. Intense Competition

Challenge: The affiliate marketing landscape is highly

competitive. With countless affiliates vying for the attention of a limited audience, it can be challenging to stand out and secure your share of the market.

Solution: Differentiation is key. Focus on a unique angle within your niche, provide valuable content, and establish your authority. For instance, if you're in the fitness niche, instead of targeting generic keywords like "weight loss tips," narrow it down to "weight loss tips for new moms" or "weight loss strategies for seniors."

2. Adapting to Algorithm Changes

Challenge: Search engines and social media platforms frequently update their algorithms, which can impact your website's visibility and traffic.

Solution: Stay informed about algorithm updates and adjust your SEO and content strategies accordingly. Diversify your traffic sources, so you're not overly reliant on a single platform. Additionally, focus on evergreen content that remains relevant over time.

3. Maintaining Consistency

Challenge: Consistency in content creation and promotion is crucial for affiliate success, but it can be challenging to maintain, especially for those managing affiliate marketing alongside other commitments.

Solution: Create a content calendar and schedule content in advance. Repurpose and update older content to save time. Consider outsourcing tasks like content writing or social media management to maintain a steady flow of content.

4. Compliance and Legal Issues

Challenge: Affiliate marketers must adhere to regulations and disclose affiliate relationships transparently. Failure to do so can lead to legal issues.

Solution: Familiarize yourself with relevant laws and regulations, such as the FTC guidelines in the United States. Clearly disclose your affiliate relationships in a conspicuous and honest manner. It's better to err on the side of caution when it comes to compliance.

5. Affiliate Program Changes

Challenge: Affiliate programs may change their terms, commission structures, or even shut down, affecting your income.

Solution: Regularly monitor program terms and conditions. Diversify your affiliate partnerships to reduce reliance on a single program. Be prepared to adapt and seek new opportunities if a program no longer aligns with your goals.

6. Burnout and Overwhelm

Challenge: Managing an affiliate marketing business can be demanding, leading to burnout and overwhelm.

Solution: Prioritize self-care and time management. Set realistic goals and avoid overextending yourself. Consider outsourcing or delegating tasks when feasible.

7. Inconsistent Earnings

Challenge: Affiliate marketing income can be inconsistent, with fluctuations from month to month.

Solution: Create multiple income streams within your affiliate business. This can include diversifying your product promotions, exploring different niches, or offering additional services related to your niche.

Remember that challenges are a natural part of any entrepreneurial endeavor, and affiliate marketing is no exception. Each challenge presents an opportunity for growth and learning. By staying informed, remaining adaptable, and implementing effective strategies, you can overcome these obstacles and emerge as a triumphant affiliate marketer, achieving your goals and realizing your full potential in the affiliate marketing landscape.

7.3.2 Staying Motivated: Fueling Your Affiliate Marketing Journey

Affiliate marketing, like any entrepreneurial pursuit, is a journey filled with highs and lows. Throughout this journey, your level of motivation plays a pivotal role in your ability to overcome obstacles and achieve your goals. In this section, we'll delve into the significance of staying motivated in affiliate marketing and explore strategies to keep your motivation consistently high, even when faced with challenges.

The Importance of Motivation

Motivation is the driving force behind your affiliate marketing endeavors. It's what propels you to create valuable content, engage with your audience, and seek out new opportunities. Without motivation, your efforts may wane, and you might find it challenging to maintain consistency and enthusiasm in your affiliate marketing business.

Strategies for Staying Motivated

1. **Set Clear and Inspiring Goals:** Define precise and inspiring affiliate marketing goals that align with your aspirations and dreams. Clear goals, whether related to income milestones or helping others, can reignite your passion and motivation.
2. **Break Down Goals into Achievable Steps:** Avoid feeling overwhelmed by breaking large goals into smaller, manageable steps. Each small achievement acts as a stepping stone toward your larger objectives, keeping you motivated as you make consistent progress.

3. **Celebrate Your Wins:** Recognize and celebrate your accomplishments along the way, rather than waiting until you reach your ultimate goal. Milestones such as subscriber milestones or successful negotiations deserve acknowledgment and can boost your motivation.

4. **Stay Informed and Adapt:** Stay informed about industry trends and changes in affiliate marketing. Knowledge empowers you and keeps your motivation fueled, enabling you to adapt your strategies effectively in the evolving landscape.

5. **Connect with Like-Minded Individuals:** Combat the solitude of affiliate marketing by engaging with online communities and networking events where you can connect with fellow marketers. Sharing experiences, challenges, and successes with peers can provide valuable insights and enhance your motivation.

6. **Visualize Your Success:** Take time to visualize your success, imagining the achievement of your goals and the positive impact it will have on your life. Visualization reinforces your commitment and helps maintain strong motivation.

7. **Stay Disciplined:** Combine motivation with discipline by creating and adhering to a schedule, even when motivation wanes. Consistently working toward your goals, regardless of how you feel, can rekindle your motivation.

8. **Learn from Challenges:** Embrace challenges and setbacks as opportunities for growth. Instead of viewing them as obstacles, analyze what went wrong, learn from the experience, and use it to fuel your motivation to improve.

9. **Remember Your "Why":** Reflect on the reasons that initially drove you to start your affiliate marketing journey. Reconnecting with your "why," whether it's financial freedom, helping others, or pursuing

your passion, can reignite your determination and motivation.

In the ever-evolving world of affiliate marketing, staying motivated is not just a luxury—it's a necessity. By incorporating these strategies into your affiliate marketing journey, you can maintain a high level of motivation, navigate challenges with resilience, and ultimately triumph as a successful affiliate marketer. Your journey may have its ups and downs, but with unwavering motivation, you'll continue to move forward toward your goals and aspirations.

7.3.3 Learning and Adaptation: Thriving in the Affiliate Marketing Evolution

In the realm of affiliate marketing, adaptability and a thirst for knowledge are your most potent weapons. The digital landscape is in constant flux, and what works today may not yield the same results tomorrow. Therefore, in this section, we'll explore the critical importance of continuous learning and adaptation in your affiliate marketing journey, along with practical strategies to keep your skills sharp and stay ahead of the curve.

The Imperative of Lifelong Learning

Affiliate marketing is a dynamic field where strategies, algorithms, and consumer behaviors undergo frequent changes. What was effective a year ago might now be outdated. To thrive in this ever-evolving landscape, you must embrace a mindset of lifelong learning. Here's why it matters:

1. **Stay Current with Industry Trends**: Keeping abreast of the latest trends and developments in affiliate marketing is vital. This knowledge empowers you to adjust your strategies, adopt new technologies, and seize emerging opportunities.

2. **Adapt to Algorithm Changes**: Search engines and social media platforms continually update

their algorithms. Understanding these changes and adapting your content and SEO strategies accordingly is crucial for maintaining visibility and traffic.

3. **Competitive Advantage**: Continuous learning can give you a competitive edge. By staying ahead of your competitors, you position yourself as a leader in your niche, attracting more followers and potential customers.

4. **Optimize Your Efforts**: Learning allows you to fine-tune your marketing efforts. You can identify what's working and what isn't, helping you allocate your time and resources more efficiently.

5. **Enhance Audience Engagement**: Understanding consumer behavior and preferences is paramount. This knowledge enables you to create content and offers that resonate with your audience, leading to higher engagement and conversions.

Strategies for Continuous Learning and Adaptation

1. **Stay Informed through Industry Sources**: Keep up with the latest trends, algorithm updates, and case studies by regularly reading trusted affiliate marketing blogs, news websites, and industry publications.

2. **Attend Webinars, Conferences, and Online Courses**: Participate in webinars and conferences hosted by industry experts and enroll in relevant online courses. These opportunities offer valuable insights, networking, and skill development.

3. **Engage in Networking and Experimentation**: Join online forums, social media groups, and networking events to connect with fellow affiliate marketers. Experiment with new strategies, A/B testing, and data-driven decision-making to refine your approach.

4. **Seek Mentorship and Expert Guidance**: Find a mentor or coach experienced in affiliate marketing to

accelerate your learning and avoid common pitfalls. Their guidance and feedback can significantly impact your success.

5. **Leverage Subscription Services and Analytics Tools:** Subscribe to industry newsletters, podcasts, and YouTube channels to access expert knowledge and experiences. Utilize analytics tools like Google Analytics, SEMrush, and Moz to monitor your website's performance and user behavior.

6. **Embrace an Adaptation Mindset:** Cultivate a mindset that welcomes change and views it as an opportunity for growth. Be flexible and adjust your strategies when algorithms shift or trends evolve to remain competitive.

7. **Stay Ethical and Compliant:** While adapting, prioritize ethical marketing practices and compliance with regulations. Building trust with your audience is paramount for long-term success in affiliate marketing.

In the affiliate marketing arena, success belongs to those who are nimble, willing to evolve, and committed to continuous learning. By integrating these strategies into your affiliate marketing journey, you not only ensure your relevance in a competitive landscape but also position yourself for sustained success and growth. The affiliate marketing world will continue to evolve, and with the right mindset and strategies, you can not only keep pace but thrive in this dynamic field.

7.3.4 Overcoming Plateaus: Breathing New Life into Your Affiliate Marketing Business

Plateaus are a common challenge in the affiliate marketing journey. They're those frustrating periods when your progress seems to stall, and your efforts yield diminishing returns. However, rest assured that plateaus are not the end of the road. In this section, we'll delve into the art of identifying and overcoming plateaus in affiliate marketing, providing you with effective techniques to breathe new life into your affiliate business.

Recognizing the Plateau

Identifying a plateau is the first step towards overcoming it. Here are some signs that you might be experiencing a plateau in your affiliate marketing business:

1. **Stagnant Earnings**: Your affiliate earnings have remained relatively flat for an extended period, despite consistent efforts.
2. **Declining Traffic**: Your website's traffic is dwindling, and you're struggling to attract new visitors or retain existing ones.
3. **Conversion Rate Drop**: Your conversion rate, which measures the percentage of visitors who take the desired action (e.g., making a purchase), is declining.
4. **Content Fatigue**: You've exhausted your content ideas, and your audience engagement is waning.
5. **Lack of Innovation**: You're sticking to the same strategies and not exploring new approaches or technologies.

Techniques for Overcoming Plateaus

1. **Content Refresh and Diversification:** Revamp your content by updating existing articles and diversifying content formats to include videos, infographics, podcasts, or interactive elements. This can re-engage your audience and improve your SEO rankings.
2. **Keyword Strategy Review:** Reevaluate your keyword strategy with fresh research to identify trending topics and queries relevant to your niche. Adapting your keywords can help attract new audiences.
3. **Competitor Analysis and Skill Development:** Analyze successful affiliates in your niche to identify different

approaches and adapt their strategies as needed. Additionally, invest in skill development through courses, webinars, and mentors to enhance your affiliate marketing expertise.

4. **Audience Engagement and Feedback:** Solicit feedback from your audience through surveys, comments, and social media interactions to better understand their needs and preferences. Engaging with your audience can help you tailor your content and promotions more effectively.

5. **Networking and Niche Expansion:** Reconnect with your affiliate marketing network to gain fresh insights and collaborative opportunities. Consider expanding into related niches to diversify your revenue streams and discover new growth avenues.

6. **Traffic Source Diversification:** Explore alternative traffic sources to reduce reliance on a single platform or channel. Diversifying your traffic can safeguard against algorithm changes and market fluctuations.

7. **A/B Testing and Data-Driven Decisions:** Implement A/B testing to refine your strategies, including calls to action, landing pages, and content layouts. Use data and analytics to make informed decisions and optimize your affiliate marketing efforts.

8. **Patience, Persistence, and Goal Setting:** Recognize that plateaus are part of the journey and may take time to overcome. Stay patient and persistent, setting new goals to reignite your motivation and sense of purpose in affiliate marketing.

9. **Ethical and Sustainable Practices:** Ensure that your affiliate marketing business is built on sustainable and ethical practices. Building trust with your audience is crucial for long-term success.

Remember that overcoming plateaus is a natural part of any entrepreneurial journey, including affiliate marketing. It's a chance to reevaluate, adapt, and emerge stronger. By implementing these techniques and maintaining a growth mindset, you can not only break through plateaus but also achieve sustained success in the dynamic world of affiliate marketing.

CHAPTER 8: ADVANCED AFFILIATE STRATEGIES

As you progress in your affiliate marketing journey, you'll find that the landscape continually evolves, presenting new opportunities and challenges. In this section, we delve into advanced affiliate strategies that go beyond the basics, equipping you with the knowledge and tactics needed to thrive in a competitive environment. From harnessing the power of email marketing to data-driven decision-making, these strategies will elevate your affiliate marketing game to the next level.

8.1 Power of Email Marketing

Email marketing is a potent tool in the affiliate marketer's arsenal, offering a direct and personalized way to engage with your audience. In this section, we explore the transformative power of email marketing within the affiliate landscape. From building and nurturing your email list to crafting compelling email campaigns, you'll discover how to harness the full potential of this channel to drive affiliate success.

8.1.1 Email Marketing Essentials: The Foundation of Affiliate Success

Email marketing is not just a valuable component of affiliate marketing; it's a foundational strategy that can significantly enhance your affiliate earnings. In this section, we'll explore the fundamental principles of email marketing in the context of affiliate marketing and how building and nurturing an email list can be a game-changer for your affiliate endeavors.

Understanding the Power of Email Marketing

At its core, email marketing is about creating a direct and personal connection with your audience. Unlike social media or other online platforms, your email list is a digital asset that you own. This means you have full control over how you communicate with your subscribers, making it a reliable and consistent channel for promoting affiliate products or services.

One of the fundamental principles of email marketing is the concept of permission-based marketing. This approach involves sending emails only to individuals who have willingly subscribed to receive them. It's not about spamming people's inboxes but rather establishing a mutually beneficial relationship with your audience. Subscribers opt-in because they trust your content and value the insights and recommendations you provide.

The Power of Building and Nurturing an Email List

Your email list is a community of individuals who have shown interest in your niche, content, and recommendations. It's a highly targeted audience that can be more receptive to your affiliate promotions than casual website visitors. Here's how building and nurturing your email list can enhance your affiliate earnings:

1. **Audience Trust:** Subscribers on your email list have already expressed trust in your expertise and opinions. They are more likely to consider your recommendations seriously because they value the insights you provide.
2. **Targeted Promotions:** Email allows you to segment

your audience based on their interests, behavior, or demographics. This means you can tailor your affiliate promotions to specific segments, increasing relevance and conversion rates.

3. **Repeat Engagements:** Email marketing enables you to have multiple touchpoints with your audience. You can send a series of emails to nurture leads, educate subscribers, and gradually introduce them to affiliate products or services.

4. **Long-Term Relationships:** Unlike one-off website visitors, email subscribers can become long-term followers and customers. A well-nurtured email list can yield affiliate commissions not just today but for months or even years to come.

5. **Measurable Results:** Email marketing platforms provide robust analytics, allowing you to track open rates, click-through rates, conversion rates, and more. This data helps you refine your email marketing strategy for better results.

In affiliate marketing, transparency and authenticity are crucial. Always disclose your affiliate relationships in your email communications. Honesty builds trust with your audience, and when subscribers know you're upfront about your affiliations and recommend products or services you genuinely believe in, they are more likely to take action based on your recommendations.

As we progress through this section, we'll delve deeper into the strategies and tactics that can help you become an email marketing expert in the world of affiliate marketing. From crafting compelling email campaigns to measuring their effectiveness, you'll gain the tools and knowledge to make email marketing a powerful ally in your affiliate endeavors.

8.1.2 Crafting Effective Affiliate Emails: Driving Engagement and Conversions

Creating compelling affiliate emails is an art and science that can significantly impact your affiliate marketing success. In this section, we'll explore the strategies and techniques to help you craft emails that not only captivate your subscribers but also drive higher open rates, click-through rates, and conversions.

Understanding the Email Marketing Funnel

Before delving into crafting effective affiliate emails, it's essential to grasp the concept of the email marketing funnel. This funnel represents the stages your subscribers go through, from being aware of your email list to becoming loyal customers. Here are the key stages:

1. **Awareness:** Subscribers join your email list, often through lead magnets or sign-up forms on your website. At this stage, they are becoming familiar with your brand and content.
2. **Interest:** Subscribers show a deeper interest by opening and engaging with your emails. They are seeking valuable insights and information from you.
3. **Consideration:** Subscribers consider your recommendations and affiliate offers. They may click on affiliate links and explore products or services.
4. **Conversion:** Subscribers make a purchase through your affiliate links, becoming customers of the promoted products or services.
5. **Loyalty:** Some customers continue to engage with your content and become repeat buyers or loyal followers.

Crafting effective affiliate emails involves tailoring your content to each stage of this funnel. Let's delve into strategies for each stage:

1. Awareness Stage: Engaging Welcome Emails
- Start with a warm and engaging welcome email series

for new subscribers. This series can introduce them to your brand, your niche, and what they can expect from your emails.

2. Interest Stage: Value-Packed Content

- Focus on providing value to your subscribers. Share informative articles, how-to guides, and insights related to your niche. Keep your content relevant and engaging to maintain their interest.

3. Consideration Stage: Introducing Affiliate Offers

- Gradually introduce affiliate offers in your emails, but don't rush. Ensure that the products or services align with your subscribers' interests and needs. Explain the benefits and how they can solve specific problems.

4. Conversion Stage: Persuasive Call to Action

- When promoting affiliate products, craft persuasive calls to action (CTAs). Highlight the value, benefits, and any special offers or discounts. Use compelling language and visuals to encourage clicks.

5. Loyalty Stage: Building Trust

- After conversions, continue nurturing the relationship with your customers. Share product updates, additional resources, and exclusive offers. Building trust can lead to repeat purchases and brand advocacy.

Strategies for Crafting Effective Affiliate Emails

- **Subject Lines:** Your subject line is the first thing subscribers see. Craft attention-grabbing, relevant, and curiosity-inducing subject lines to increase open rates.
- **Personalization:** Use subscribers' names and segment your list to send targeted content. Personalized emails tend to perform better.
- **Compelling Content:** Create engaging and valuable content that resonates with your audience. Tell stories,

solve problems, and provide actionable insights.

- **Visuals:** Incorporate eye-catching visuals, such as images and videos, to make your emails more appealing.
- **Mobile Optimization:** Ensure your emails are mobile-responsive since many subscribers access emails on their mobile devices.
- **Testing:** A/B test various elements of your emails, including subject lines, content, CTAs, and visuals, to identify what works best for your audience.
- **Frequency:** Find the right balance between sending enough emails to stay top-of-mind and not overwhelming your subscribers with too many messages.
- **Tracking and Analytics:** Use email marketing platforms' analytics to measure open rates, click-through rates, and conversions. Analyze this data to refine your email strategy.

Effective affiliate emails should provide value, build trust, and guide subscribers toward making informed purchasing decisions. When done well, they can be a powerful tool for driving engagement and conversions in your affiliate marketing efforts.

8.1.3 Automation and Segmentation: Enhancing Email Marketing Efficiency

In affiliate marketing, where managing a growing list of subscribers and promoting various products or services is essential, email automation and list segmentation are indispensable tools. These advanced email marketing techniques not only enhance efficiency but also deliver more personalized and targeted content to your audience.

Understanding Email Automation

Email automation refers to the use of technology to send emails automatically based on predefined triggers or conditions. This eliminates the need for manual intervention, allowing you to engage with your audience consistently and timely. Here's how automation can benefit your affiliate marketing efforts:

1. Workflow Automation: Create email workflows that trigger specific emails based on subscriber actions or behaviors. For example, you can set up a workflow that sends a welcome email immediately after someone subscribes, followed by a series of educational emails and then promotional emails as they progress through the email marketing funnel.

2. Drip Campaigns: Drip campaigns are a type of email automation that sends a series of emails to subscribers at predetermined intervals. This is particularly useful for nurturing leads, introducing affiliate offers gradually, and providing value over time.

3. Abandoned Cart Recovery: If you're promoting e-commerce products, automated emails can help recover abandoned carts by sending reminder emails to potential buyers who added items to their cart but didn't complete the purchase.

4. Personalization: Automation allows you to personalize emails based on subscriber data, such as their name, location, past purchases, and browsing behavior. Personalized emails tend to have higher engagement rates.

List Segmentation for Targeted Content

List segmentation involves dividing your email list into smaller, more targeted groups based on specific criteria. This allows you to send highly relevant content to different segments of your audience. Here's how list segmentation can boost your affiliate marketing efforts:

1. Improved Relevance: By segmenting your list, you can tailor your email content to the interests and preferences of each group. Subscribers are more likely to engage with content that directly relates to their needs.

2. Higher Open and Click-Through Rates: Segmented email campaigns often result in higher open and click-through rates because subscribers receive content that aligns with their interests.

3. Better Conversions: When subscribers receive content that resonates with them, it increases the likelihood of conversions. Whether you're promoting products or providing valuable information, segmentation can lead to more affiliate earnings.

4. Reduced Unsubscribes: Targeted emails are less likely to annoy subscribers because they receive content that's relevant to them. This can help reduce unsubscribes and maintain a healthy email list.

Implementing Automation and Segmentation

To leverage email automation and list segmentation effectively:

- Choose a reputable email marketing platform that offers robust automation and segmentation features. Popular options include Mailchimp, AWeber, ConvertKit, and more.
- Define clear goals and objectives for your automated campaigns and segmented lists. Determine what actions or behaviors will trigger specific emails.
- Segment your email list based on relevant criteria, such as demographics, purchase history, engagement level, or any other factors that align with your affiliate marketing strategy.
- Craft personalized and targeted content for each segment, ensuring that it addresses their specific needs and interests.
- Test and optimize your automated workflows and segmented campaigns regularly to improve performance.

- Monitor key metrics, including open rates, click-through rates, conversion rates, and revenue generated, to gauge the effectiveness of your efforts.

In conclusion, email automation and list segmentation are powerful tools that can take your affiliate marketing to the next level. They enable you to deliver more personalized, timely, and relevant content to your subscribers, ultimately leading to higher engagement, conversions, and affiliate earnings.

8.2 Social Media Tactics

In today's digital landscape, social media has become a cornerstone of affiliate marketing success. Leveraging the power of social media platforms can help affiliates reach a broader audience, engage with potential customers, and drive affiliate conversions. This section will delve into a range of effective social media tactics tailored to maximize your affiliate marketing endeavors.

8.2.1 Leveraging Social Platforms

In the realm of advanced affiliate marketing, social media platforms emerge as invaluable tools for affiliates looking to expand their reach and engage with their target audience on a deeper level. Understanding the role of social media in affiliate marketing and selecting the most suitable platforms are fundamental steps toward optimizing your affiliate strategies.

The Social Media Landscape in Affiliate Marketing

Social media platforms have evolved into bustling hubs of online activity, drawing in billions of users worldwide. These platforms provide affiliates with an expansive playground to showcase products and services, share valuable content, and foster connections with potential customers. When utilized effectively, social media can drive significant traffic to your affiliate offerings and fuel your monetization efforts.

Selecting the Right Social Media Platforms

Not all social media platforms are created equal, and each has its unique audience, features, and strengths. To harness the power of social media for your affiliate marketing endeavors, it's crucial to choose the platforms that align with your niche, target audience, and promotional content. Here's a glimpse of some prominent social platforms and their affiliate marketing potential:

1. **Facebook**: As one of the largest social networks, Facebook offers a diverse audience and robust advertising tools. Affiliates can create niche-specific pages, engage in groups, and run targeted ad campaigns.
2. **Instagram**: With its visual focus, Instagram is ideal for affiliates promoting products or services with strong visual appeal. Instagram influencers, stories, and shoppable posts can boost conversions.
3. **Twitter**: Twitter's fast-paced nature suits affiliates sharing news, updates, and timely promotions. Leveraging hashtags and engaging with trending topics can amplify your reach.
4. **Pinterest**: Pinterest is a visual discovery platform that works well for affiliates in niches like fashion, home decor, and DIY. Creating and sharing visually appealing pins can drive traffic to affiliate links.
5. **LinkedIn**: For affiliates in B2B niches, LinkedIn offers a professional network to connect with businesses and decision-makers. Publishing articles and participating in relevant groups can be effective.
6. **YouTube**: Video content reigns supreme on YouTube, making it an excellent platform for affiliates who can create informative and engaging video reviews, tutorials, and product showcases.
7. **TikTok**: This rapidly growing platform is perfect for

affiliates targeting a younger demographic. Short-form videos can quickly capture attention and direct users to affiliate products.

Tailoring Your Approach

While these platforms hold great potential, success on social media hinges on a well-thought-out strategy. It's essential to tailor your approach to each platform, considering the type of content that resonates with the audience, the frequency of posting, and engagement tactics. Moreover, staying updated with platform algorithm changes and best practices is crucial for maintaining visibility and relevance.

As we delve deeper into this section, we will explore strategies and techniques specific to each social media platform, helping you unlock the full potential of your affiliate marketing efforts in the social sphere. Get ready to harness the power of social media to boost your affiliate conversions and earnings.

8.2.2 Building a Social Media Presence

In the intricate web of advanced affiliate marketing, your social media presence becomes a pivotal factor that can either propel your affiliate ventures to new heights or leave them languishing in obscurity. Building and nurturing a strong social media presence is not just a matter of posting sporadically; it's a strategic endeavor that involves branding, content strategies, and engagement techniques. Let's embark on this journey to explore the art of crafting a compelling social media presence that captivates your audience and drives affiliate success.

The Foundations of Social Media Presence

Creating a formidable social media presence begins with a robust foundation rooted in clarity, consistency, and authenticity. Here are some strategies to lay these essential cornerstones:

1. **Define Your Brand**: Start by clearly defining your affiliate brand. What values and principles does it represent? What sets you apart from others in your niche? Establishing a distinct brand identity helps you stand out in the crowded social media landscape.
2. **Consistent Branding**: Ensure that your branding elements, such as logos, color schemes, and messaging, remain consistent across all social media platforms. Consistency breeds familiarity and trust among your audience.
3. **Content Strategy**: Develop a content strategy that aligns with your brand and resonates with your target audience. Consider the types of content that best suit your niche and audience preferences, whether it's informative blog posts, eye-catching visuals, engaging videos, or a blend of these.
4. **Content Calendar**: Implement a content calendar to maintain a consistent posting schedule. A well-structured calendar allows you to plan your content in advance, ensuring a steady flow of posts that cater to your audience's needs and interests.

Engagement Techniques

Engagement is the heartbeat of a thriving social media presence. It's not just about broadcasting content but also about fostering meaningful interactions with your audience. Here's how you can master the art of engagement:

1. **Active Participation**: Be actively involved in conversations on your social media platforms. Respond promptly to comments, messages, and mentions. Show genuine interest in your audience's questions and feedback.
2. **Ask Questions**: Encourage engagement by asking open-ended questions in your posts. This invites your

audience to share their thoughts and experiences, fostering a sense of community.

3. **Contests and Giveaways**: Periodic contests, giveaways, and challenges can spark excitement and boost engagement. Ensure that these initiatives align with your niche and affiliate offerings.

4. **User-Generated Content**: Encourage your audience to create content related to your affiliate products or services. Share and celebrate user-generated content, turning your followers into brand advocates.

Monitoring and Analytics

Building a social media presence is an ongoing endeavor that requires continuous monitoring and improvement. Leverage social media analytics tools to gain insights into your performance. Pay attention to metrics like engagement rates, follower growth, and post reach. Analyze which types of content resonate most with your audience and adjust your strategy accordingly.

The Power of Collaboration

Consider collaborating with influencers or complementary brands in your niche. Partnering with influencers can extend your reach and lend credibility to your affiliate promotions.

As you venture deeper into this section, we will delve into platform-specific strategies and explore the nuances of building a robust social media presence on various platforms like Facebook, Instagram, Twitter, and more. By the end, you'll be equipped with the knowledge and tools to craft an engaging and influential social media presence that elevates your affiliate marketing endeavors.

8.2.3 Paid Advertising on Social Media

In the realm of advanced affiliate marketing, where competition is fierce, mastering paid advertising on social media platforms becomes a powerful weapon in your arsenal. Social media advertising offers precise targeting, extensive reach, and a variety of ad formats that can amplify your affiliate promotions. Let's dive into the world of advanced social media advertising tactics and explore how to optimize ad campaigns on platforms like Facebook, Instagram, and Twitter.

The Dynamics of Advanced Social Media Advertising

Advanced social media advertising isn't just about boosting a post or creating a simple ad. It involves a strategic approach that considers various factors, from audience segmentation to ad creatives. Here's how you can navigate this landscape effectively:

1. **Audience Segmentation**: Start by defining your target audience with precision. Utilize the robust audience targeting options available on platforms like Facebook Ads Manager. Create custom audiences based on demographics, interests, behaviors, and even website visitors or email subscribers. Advanced advertisers often employ lookalike audiences to reach users similar to their existing customers.

2. **Ad Creative**: Your ad creatives play a pivotal role in capturing the attention of your audience. Invest time and resources in crafting compelling visuals and ad copy. A/B testing different ad creatives can help you identify what resonates best with your audience.

3. **Ad Formats**: Social media platforms offer a variety of ad formats, including image ads, video ads, carousel ads, and more. Experiment with different formats to see which ones yield the best results for your affiliate promotions.

4. **Ad Scheduling**: Optimize the timing of your ad campaigns by scheduling them for periods when your target audience is most active. Social media platforms provide insights into audience activity patterns, allowing you to choose optimal ad delivery times.

5. **Budget and Bidding**: Advanced advertisers often employ strategies like budget optimization and automated bidding to maximize their ad spend. These techniques help allocate your budget effectively and bid competitively for ad placements.

Retargeting and Remarketing

One of the most potent advanced tactics in social media advertising is retargeting or remarketing. This involves showing ads to users who have previously interacted with your website, content, or ads. Remarketing keeps your brand top-of-mind and encourages users to return and complete desired actions, such as making a purchase or signing up for a newsletter.

Ad Campaign Tracking and Optimization

To gauge the effectiveness of your advanced social media advertising campaigns, it's crucial to implement tracking mechanisms. Use tools like the Facebook Pixel or custom UTM parameters to monitor conversions, click-through rates, and other essential metrics. Continuously analyze campaign performance and adjust your strategies based on the data.

Scaling and Testing

As you gain experience in advanced social media advertising, consider scaling your successful campaigns. Allocate more budget to high-performing ads or replicate successful strategies across different platforms. Don't shy away from testing new ideas and approaches. A/B testing different ad elements, audiences, and objectives can unveil hidden opportunities for growth.

Compliance and Transparency

Lastly, remember that transparency and compliance are paramount in affiliate marketing. Ensure that your ads clearly disclose your affiliate relationships to maintain trust with your audience and comply with platform policies.

Advanced social media advertising in affiliate marketing is a dynamic field that requires ongoing learning and adaptation. By embracing these advanced tactics and strategies, you can harness the full potential of social media platforms to drive affiliate earnings and achieve your marketing objectives.

8.3 Data-Driven Decision-Making

In the rapidly evolving landscape of affiliate marketing, the ability to make informed decisions based on data is a game-changer. Data-driven decision-making empowers affiliate marketers to optimize their strategies, enhance their targeting, and maximize their earnings. In this section, we delve into the world of data-driven affiliate marketing, exploring how to collect, analyze, and leverage data for strategic advantage.

8.3.1 The Importance of Analytics

In the dynamic realm of affiliate marketing, staying competitive and achieving consistent success hinges significantly on the ability to harness the power of data analytics. This section delves into the paramount importance of analytics, shedding light on its pivotal role in affiliate marketing endeavors. By understanding how data-driven decisions can propel your affiliate marketing strategies to new heights, you'll be better equipped to navigate the intricate landscape of online marketing.

Why Analytics Matters in Affiliate Marketing

Affiliate marketing is no longer a hit-or-miss endeavor; it's evolved into a precise science, where every click, conversion, and engagement can be tracked and analyzed. Analytics serves as your compass in this digital landscape, helping you navigate through the vast sea of information, pinpoint opportunities, and steer clear of pitfalls.

One of the fundamental reasons why analytics is indispensable in affiliate marketing is its capacity to provide insights. Through data collection and analysis, affiliate marketers can gain deep insights into their audience's behavior, preferences, and pain points. These insights serve as the foundation for crafting highly targeted and effective marketing campaigns.

Moreover, analytics empowers you to measure the performance of your affiliate marketing efforts accurately. It's not merely about counting clicks and conversions; it's about understanding what drives those actions. Which marketing channels are most effective? What types of content resonate with your audience? What time of day sees the highest engagement? Analytics answers these questions and more.

Data-Driven Decisions for Optimization

The heart of data-driven decision-making lies in optimization. When you have access to data-backed insights, you can fine-tune your affiliate marketing strategies for maximum impact. For example, if analytics reveal that a particular product review video has a higher conversion rate than others, you can allocate more resources to create similar content. If you find that a specific demographic engages the most with your affiliate links, you can tailor your advertising campaigns to target that demographic more effectively.

Moreover, analytics isn't limited to assessing past performance; it also aids in predictive analysis. By studying historical data, you can make informed predictions about future trends and behaviors. This enables you to adapt your strategies in advance, ensuring you're always one step ahead of the competition.

In summary, analytics is the compass that guides affiliate marketers through the ever-changing landscape of online marketing. It provides valuable insights, measures performance, and empowers optimization. In the following sections, we'll explore the tools, techniques, and best practices for effective data collection and analysis in affiliate marketing. By the end of this chapter, you'll have the knowledge and tools to become a data-driven affiliate marketing expert, making decisions that are rooted in solid information and primed for success.

8.3.2 Implementing Advanced Analytics Tools for Data-Driven Decisions

In the world of affiliate marketing, data is more than just numbers; it's the compass guiding you to success. While basic analytics tools provide essential insights, advanced analytics tools take your affiliate marketing performance to a whole new level. In this section, we'll delve into the implementation of these advanced tools and provide guidance on how to use them effectively.

1. Google Analytics Enhanced E-commerce Tracking

One of the cornerstones of advanced analytics in affiliate marketing is Google Analytics Enhanced E-commerce Tracking. This feature provides in-depth insights into your affiliate website's performance regarding sales and revenue.

- **Enable Enhanced E-commerce Tracking**: Start by enabling this feature in your Google Analytics account. This involves adding a tracking code snippet to your website.
- **Set Up Enhanced E-commerce Tags**: Implement specific tags that capture data related to product impressions, clicks, add-to-carts, and purchases.
- **Custom Dimensions and Metrics**: Configure custom dimensions and metrics to track affiliate-specific data, such as clicks on affiliate links, referral sources, and affiliate-driven conversions.

2. Affiliate Tracking Software Integration

Your affiliate tracking software is the backbone of your affiliate marketing operation. These tools go beyond basic analytics and offer specialized features for tracking clicks, conversions, and commissions generated through your affiliate links.

- **Select a Reliable Affiliate Tracking Software**: Choose a reputable affiliate tracking platform that aligns with your affiliate marketing goals.
- **Integration with Your Website**: Integrate the tracking software seamlessly with your website. This often involves adding tracking code snippets or plugins.
- **Customize Tracking Parameters**: Configure tracking parameters to capture granular data, such as affiliate link clicks, campaign IDs, and conversion events.
- **Cross-Device Tracking**: Ensure that your tracking software can handle cross-device tracking to provide accurate attribution, especially in the age of mobile browsing.

3. Heatmaps and User Session Recording Tools

Understanding how users interact with your affiliate website is crucial. Heatmaps and user session recording tools offer visual representations of user behavior, helping you identify areas for improvement.

- **Choose the Right Heatmap Tool**: Select a heatmap tool that suits your needs and integrates with your website.
- **Install and Configure**: Install the heatmap tracking code on your website to start recording user interactions.
- **Analyze Click Heatmaps**: Review click heatmaps to identify which elements of your pages receive the most attention. Optimize the placement of affiliate links and call-to-action buttons accordingly.
- **Evaluate Scroll Behavior**: Study scroll heatmaps to understand how far users scroll on your content.

Ensure that essential affiliate content is visible without excessive scrolling.

- **Utilize User Session Recordings**: Watch recorded user sessions to identify user experience issues, friction points, and areas where visitors drop off. Use this data to refine your website's design and flow.

4. Split Testing and A/B Testing Tools

Split testing, often referred to as A/B testing, is a fundamental technique for optimizing affiliate marketing campaigns. These tools help you compare different variations of content or promotional strategies to determine what resonates best with your audience.

- **Select a Split Testing Tool**: Choose a split testing tool that aligns with your goals. Many email marketing platforms and website builders offer built-in A/B testing features.
- **Define Testing Objectives**: Clearly define your testing objectives, whether it's improving click-through rates on affiliate links, enhancing landing page conversions, or optimizing email open rates.
- **Create Test Variations**: Develop multiple variations of the element you want to test. This could include different headlines, calls to action, email subject lines, or landing page layouts.
- **Run Controlled Experiments**: Implement controlled experiments by splitting your audience into groups and showing each group a different variation.
- **Analyze Results**: Analyze the results of your split tests to determine which variation performs best. Implement the winning version to improve your affiliate marketing efforts.

5. SEO Analytics Tools

For affiliates reliant on organic traffic, advanced SEO analytics tools are indispensable. They provide insights into keyword performance, backlink profiles, and competitor analysis.

- **Choose SEO Analytics Software**: Invest in reputable SEO analytics software or platforms like Moz, Ahrefs, or SEMrush.
- **Keyword Rank Tracking**: Monitor your affiliate content's performance in search engine results pages (SERPs). Track keyword rankings, search volume, and click-through rates to identify optimization opportunities.
- **Backlink Analysis**: Use these tools to analyze your website's backlink profile, identify high-quality backlinks, and uncover opportunities for link building.
- **Competitor Analysis**: Conduct competitor analysis to understand competitor strategies and identify gaps and opportunities in your niche. Keep a close eye on competitors' rankings and content strategies.

By implementing these advanced analytics tools and following the provided guidance, you'll be well-equipped to gather actionable insights, optimize your affiliate marketing strategies, and maximize your earnings. Remember that consistent data analysis and refinement of your strategies based on these insights are key to achieving long-term success in affiliate marketing.

8.3.3 A/B Testing and Optimization

In the ever-evolving landscape of affiliate marketing, staying competitive and maximizing your earning potential requires a data-driven approach. One powerful method for achieving this is through A/B testing and optimization. In this section, we'll delve into the world of A/B testing, explaining its significance and providing real-world case studies that demonstrate the substantial impact it can have on your affiliate strategies.

Understanding A/B Testing

A/B testing, also known as split testing, is a systematic method of comparing two versions of a webpage, email, or marketing material to determine which one performs better. It involves dividing your audience into two groups, where one group sees the original version (A), and the other sees a modified version (B) with a specific change. By analyzing the performance metrics of each group, you can make data-driven decisions to optimize your affiliate strategies.

Case Study 1: Optimizing Email Subject Lines

Background: An affiliate marketer specializing in promoting e-commerce products through email campaigns wanted to improve their email open rates.

Strategy: They conducted an A/B test on their email subject lines. In the "A" group, they used their usual subject lines, while in the "B" group, they experimented with more personalized and attention-grabbing subject lines.

Results: The A/B test revealed that the "B" group, with the modified subject lines, experienced a 30% increase in email open rates compared to the "A" group. This change significantly improved the affiliate marketer's ability to capture the audience's attention.

Case Study 2: Landing Page Optimization

Background: An affiliate marketer with a website focused on product reviews wanted to boost their conversion rates for affiliate products.

Strategy: They conducted A/B tests on their landing pages, experimenting with different call-to-action (CTA) buttons, colors, and placements. The "A" group saw the original landing page design, while the "B" group encountered the modified version.

Results: The A/B test revealed that the "B" group's landing page, with the optimized CTA elements, achieved a 20% higher conversion rate than the "A" group. This optimization directly translated into increased affiliate commissions.

The Impact of Data-Driven Optimization

The two case studies above illustrate the tangible benefits of A/B testing and data-driven optimization in affiliate marketing. Here are some key takeaways:

1. **Improved Performance**: A/B testing helps affiliate marketers fine-tune their strategies for better results. Whether it's increasing email open rates or boosting landing page conversions, optimization directly impacts your bottom line.
2. **Enhanced User Experience**: Optimization isn't just about increasing conversions; it's also about improving the overall user experience. By aligning your content and strategies with what resonates best with your audience, you create a more engaging and satisfying experience.
3. **Competitive Advantage**: In a competitive affiliate landscape, those who leverage A/B testing and optimization gain a significant advantage. By consistently optimizing your strategies, you stay ahead of the curve and adapt to changing market dynamics.
4. **Cost-Efficiency**: A/B testing allows you to make informed changes based on data, reducing the risk of costly marketing decisions that may not yield the desired results.
5. **Continuous Improvement**: A/B testing is an iterative process. As you gather more data and insights, you can continue to refine your strategies, achieving incremental improvements over time.

In conclusion, A/B testing and data-driven optimization are not just options for affiliate marketers; they are essential tools for success. By systematically testing and refining your strategies, as demonstrated by the case studies, you can achieve significant improvements in performance, user experience, and ultimately, your affiliate earnings. Make data-driven decisions a core part of your affiliate marketing strategy, and you'll be well on your way to triumphing over the challenges of the affiliate landscape.

8.4 Navigating the Affiliate Landscape Safely

As affiliate marketing continues to thrive and evolve, it's crucial for affiliate marketers to navigate this dynamic landscape safely and ethically. In this section, we'll explore essential strategies and principles to ensure your affiliate marketing endeavors are conducted with integrity and compliance. From adhering to regulations to safeguarding your online reputation, these insights will help you navigate the affiliate world securely.

8.4.1 Staying Compliant with Regulations

In the ever-evolving landscape of affiliate marketing, adherence to regulations is paramount. Affiliate marketers must operate within the confines of established laws and guidelines to maintain trust with both consumers and regulatory authorities. Here, we delve into the significance of compliance and offer an overview of key regulations and best practices that every affiliate marketer should be aware of.

- **Importance of Compliance:** Compliance with regulations in affiliate marketing is not merely a legal requirement; it's the foundation of a trustworthy and sustainable affiliate business. It ensures transparency, protects consumers, and upholds the integrity of the industry. By following the rules, affiliate marketers can build a positive reputation and establish long-term partnerships with merchants and networks.

- **Key Regulations:** Understanding and adhering to the

following regulations is crucial for affiliate marketers:

- **Federal Trade Commission (FTC) Guidelines:** In the United States, the FTC mandates that affiliate marketers must disclose their affiliate relationships clearly and conspicuously in their content. This includes using phrases like "affiliate link" or "commission earned" to inform users of potential financial incentives.
- **General Data Protection Regulation (GDPR):** If your affiliate marketing activities involve targeting European audiences, you must comply with GDPR regulations. This means obtaining explicit consent for data collection, ensuring data protection, and respecting user privacy rights.
- **CAN-SPAM Act:** If email marketing is part of your strategy, understanding the CAN-SPAM Act is crucial. It requires accurate sender information, opt-out mechanisms, and compliance with users' requests to unsubscribe from email lists.

- **Best Practices:** In addition to regulatory requirements, several best practices contribute to compliance and ethical affiliate marketing:

  - **Transparent Disclosures:** Always disclose your affiliate relationships clearly and honestly to your audience. Use language that is easy to understand, and ensure the disclosure is placed where users can easily spot it.
  - **Truthful Promotions:** Ensure that your promotions are accurate and truthful. Avoid making false claims about products or services you're promoting.
  - **Ethical SEO Practices:** If you're using SEO to attract traffic, adhere to ethical SEO practices. Avoid keyword stuffing, cloaking, and other

black-hat techniques.

- ◦ **Respect User Data:** If you collect user data, prioritize data protection and user consent. Be transparent about your data collection practices.
- ◦ **Stay Informed:** Regulations can change, so it's essential to stay informed about the latest developments in affiliate marketing laws. Join industry forums, follow regulatory updates, and seek legal advice if necessary.

By prioritizing compliance and ethical practices, affiliate marketers can build a strong and reputable presence in the industry while safeguarding their businesses from potential legal issues. In the next sections, we'll explore additional strategies for sustaining success and maintaining motivation in affiliate marketing.

8.4.2 Avoiding Affiliate Marketing Pitfalls

While affiliate marketing offers numerous opportunities for success, it's not without its share of pitfalls and risks. Affiliate marketers must navigate these challenges to build sustainable businesses and maintain clean reputations. In this section, we'll delve into common pitfalls and offer strategies for mitigating risks.

- • **Deceptive Practices:** One of the most significant pitfalls in affiliate marketing is the temptation to engage in deceptive practices to drive sales. This includes creating false claims about products, using misleading advertisements, or employing clickbait tactics. Such practices may lead to short-term gains but can damage your credibility and lead to legal consequences.
  - ◦ **Mitigation Strategy:** Stay committed to ethical marketing practices. Always provide accurate information about the products

or services you're promoting. Honesty and transparency build trust with your audience, fostering long-term relationships.

- **Overemphasis on Earnings:** While affiliate marketing can be lucrative, focusing solely on earnings can lead to pitfalls. Some affiliate marketers become overly aggressive, promoting products solely for commissions, which can alienate their audience.
  - **Mitigation Strategy:** Balance your focus between earnings and providing value to your audience. Prioritize products or services that genuinely align with your niche and audience's needs. Your content should always aim to educate, entertain, or solve problems, with earnings as a byproduct.

- **Ignoring Compliance:** Neglecting regulatory compliance, such as the FTC guidelines, GDPR, or CAN-SPAM Act, is a significant risk. Failure to comply with these regulations can result in legal actions, fines, and damage to your reputation.
  - **Mitigation Strategy:** Stay informed about relevant regulations in your target markets. Implement clear and conspicuous disclosures about your affiliate relationships. Regularly review and update your compliance practices as regulations evolve.

- **Dependence on a Single Traffic Source:** Relying too heavily on a single traffic source, such as organic search traffic or social media, can be risky. Algorithm changes or platform policies can disrupt your traffic flow overnight.
  - **Mitigation Strategy:** Diversify your traffic sources to reduce risk. Explore various channels like paid advertising, email

marketing, and social media. This diversification can provide a safety net if one traffic source experiences a downturn.

- **Failure to Adapt:** The affiliate marketing landscape is dynamic, with constant changes in consumer behavior, technology, and industry trends. Sticking to outdated strategies without adaptation can lead to stagnation.
  - ◦ **Mitigation Strategy:** Stay informed about industry developments and be willing to adapt. Continuously test new strategies, embrace emerging technologies, and monitor the performance of your affiliate efforts. Learning from failures and successes is essential for long-term growth.

- **Inadequate Tracking and Analysis:** Neglecting to track and analyze your affiliate marketing performance can result in missed opportunities for optimization and growth.
  - ◦ **Mitigation Strategy:** Invest in robust tracking tools and regularly review your data. Analyze key performance indicators (KPIs) to identify areas for improvement. A data-driven approach allows you to make informed decisions and optimize your strategies.

By understanding these common pitfalls and implementing mitigation strategies, affiliate marketers can not only avoid potential setbacks but also build strong and sustainable affiliate businesses. The ability to adapt, prioritize ethics, and maintain compliance will be crucial in navigating the dynamic world of affiliate marketing successfully.

8.5 Sustaining Motivation

Sustaining motivation in affiliate marketing is a critical

factor in achieving long-term success. Affiliate marketers often encounter challenges, setbacks, and moments of self-doubt on their journey. In this section, we will explore strategies and techniques to help you maintain high levels of motivation throughout your affiliate marketing career.

8.5.1 Overcoming Burnout

In the fast-paced world of advanced affiliate marketing, the risk of burnout is a common challenge that many marketers face. Burnout can result from continuous work pressure, relentless competition, and the demand for constant innovation. In this section, we will explore the concept of burnout in affiliate marketing and offer practical strategies to prevent it and recover from it effectively.

Understanding Affiliate Marketing Burnout

Affiliate marketing is known for its flexibility and potential for financial freedom, but it also comes with its unique set of stressors. Constantly striving to create quality content, manage multiple campaigns, and adapt to the evolving landscape can take a toll on affiliate marketers. Burnout can manifest in various ways, including decreased motivation, increased stress levels, and diminished creativity.

Preventing Burnout

1. **Set Realistic Goals:** One of the primary causes of burnout is setting overly ambitious goals. While ambition is essential, it's equally important to set achievable milestones. This prevents the feeling of being overwhelmed by unrealistic expectations.
2. **Time Management:** Efficient time management is crucial in preventing burnout. Create a structured work schedule that allows for regular breaks and time for relaxation. Balance your work hours with personal time to recharge.

3. **Diversify Your Efforts:** Relying on a single niche or marketing strategy can become monotonous. Diversify your efforts by exploring new niches, testing different marketing channels, and collaborating with others in the field. This variety can keep your work exciting and reduce the risk of burnout.

4. **Delegate Tasks:** As your affiliate marketing business grows, consider delegating tasks that can be handled by others. This could include outsourcing content creation, hiring a virtual assistant, or collaborating with freelancers. Delegating allows you to focus on strategic aspects of your business.

5. **Stay Informed:** The affiliate marketing landscape is constantly evolving. Staying informed about industry trends, algorithm changes, and new tools can help you adapt more effectively, reducing stress caused by unexpected shifts.

Recovering from Burnout

If you've already experienced burnout, it's essential to address it promptly to prevent long-term negative effects on your affiliate marketing career.

1. **Take a Break:** Sometimes, the best solution to burnout is a temporary break. Step away from your work, disconnect from digital devices, and engage in activities that rejuvenate your mind and body.

2. **Reflect and Adjust:** Use your break as an opportunity to reflect on what led to burnout. Were you overextending yourself? Did you have an unhealthy work-life balance? Make adjustments to your work habits and routines based on your reflections.

3. **Seek Support:** Don't hesitate to reach out to fellow affiliate marketers or mentors who may have experienced burnout themselves. They can provide valuable insights and advice on how to recover and

prevent burnout in the future.

4. **Practice Self-Care:** Self-care is essential for sustaining motivation and avoiding burnout. Incorporate activities like exercise, meditation, and hobbies into your daily routine to promote overall well-being.

Remember that burnout is not a sign of weakness; it's a common challenge in the affiliate marketing industry. By recognizing the signs, taking preventive measures, and seeking support when needed, you can overcome burnout and continue to thrive in your affiliate marketing journey.

8.5.2 Goal Setting for Continued Success

Sustaining motivation and enthusiasm in advanced affiliate marketing is a crucial aspect of achieving continued success in this dynamic field. Over time, it's natural for your initial drive to wane, and that's why setting new goals and milestones is essential to keep your affiliate marketing journey exciting and fulfilling.

The Importance of Setting New Goals

1. **Maintaining Focus:** Setting new goals allows you to maintain a clear sense of direction in your affiliate marketing endeavors. When you have specific objectives to work towards, you're less likely to lose sight of your purpose.

2. **Measuring Progress:** Goals provide a benchmark for measuring your progress. They help you track your achievements and celebrate your successes, no matter how small. This can boost your motivation by giving you a sense of accomplishment.

3. **Adapting to Change:** The affiliate marketing landscape is ever-evolving. Setting new goals enables you to adapt to changes and stay relevant. It encourages you to explore new niches, technologies, and strategies.

Strategies for Setting and Achieving Goals

1. **SMART Goals:** Use the SMART (Specific, Measurable, Achievable, Relevant, Time-bound) criteria when setting goals. This framework ensures that your goals are well-defined and realistic. For example, instead of a vague goal like "increase earnings," set a SMART goal like "increase monthly earnings by 20% in the next six months."
2. **Break Goals into Milestones:** Large goals can be overwhelming. Break them down into smaller, manageable milestones. Achieving these milestones provides a sense of progress and keeps you motivated.
3. **Regularly Review and Adjust:** Review your goals periodically. If you find that a goal is no longer relevant or achievable, don't hesitate to adjust it. Flexibility in goal-setting is essential for long-term success.
4. **Stay Accountable:** Share your goals with a trusted friend, mentor, or fellow affiliate marketer. Being accountable to someone else can motivate you to work towards your goals consistently.
5. **Reward Yourself:** Celebrate your achievements, even the small ones. Rewards can serve as positive reinforcement and enhance your motivation.

Sustaining Long-Term Motivation

1. **Continuous Learning:** Keep the flame of motivation alive by embracing a mindset of continuous learning. Stay curious about new affiliate marketing strategies, technologies, and industry trends.
2. **Networking:** Engage with other affiliate marketers, attend industry events, and participate in online forums or communities. Networking can provide fresh perspectives and inspiration.
3. **Revisit Your Why:** Reflect on why you started

your affiliate marketing journey in the first place. Reconnecting with your initial motivations can reignite your passion.

4. **Take Breaks:** Don't forget to give yourself permission to take breaks when needed. Stepping away from work periodically can help prevent burnout and renew your motivation.

5. **Visualization:** Visualize your goals and imagine the satisfaction of achieving them. Visualization can be a powerful tool for staying motivated.

Remember that motivation is not a constant state but rather a fluctuating energy that requires ongoing nurturing. By setting new goals, following effective strategies, and prioritizing self-care, you can sustain your motivation and continue to thrive in the world of advanced affiliate marketing.

CONCLUSION

In conclusion, your journey through the world of affiliate marketing has been an exploration of strategies, tactics, and principles that can lead to success in this dynamic field. We've covered a wide range of topics, from understanding the affiliate marketing ecosystem to crafting compelling content, navigating challenges, and sustaining motivation. Let's take a moment to recap key takeaways and offer some encouraging words as you move forward in your affiliate marketing endeavors.

Recap of Key Takeaways:

1. **Niche Selection:** Choosing the right niche is foundational. It's essential to align your interests and passions with market demand to maximize your affiliate marketing success.
2. **Affiliate Programs:** Select diverse, reputable affiliate programs that match your niche. Consider product alignment, commission structures, and program terms.
3. **Content Creation:** Quality content is at the core of affiliate marketing. Focus on providing value, building authority, and engaging your target audience.
4. **Traffic Generation:** Understand the different sources of web traffic, target your ideal audience, and leverage strategies like SEO, social media, and paid advertising to attract visitors.
5. **Monetization Strategies:** Beyond affiliate links,

explore various monetization methods while prioritizing user experience.

6. **Tracking and Optimization:** Implement analytics tools, monitor key metrics, and optimize your strategies based on data-driven insights.

7. **Scaling and Growth:** As you gain experience, consider scaling your efforts through outsourcing, automation, and strategic expansion.

8. **Overcoming Challenges:** Be prepared to face common challenges in affiliate marketing, such as compliance, burnout, and plateaus. Stay motivated and adapt to changes.

Encouragement for Your Affiliate Marketing Journey:

Embarking on an affiliate marketing journey is an exciting endeavor, but it's important to remember that success often comes with time and persistence. Here are some encouraging words to keep in mind:

1. **Continuous Learning:** The world of affiliate marketing is ever-evolving. Stay curious and committed to learning. New opportunities and strategies emerge regularly.

2. **Resilience:** Challenges are part of the journey. Embrace setbacks as opportunities for growth and learning. Keep moving forward, adapting, and refining your approach.

3. **Networking:** Connect with fellow affiliate marketers, mentors, and industry experts. Networking can provide valuable insights, support, and inspiration.

4. **Goal Setting:** Set clear, achievable goals to guide your efforts. Regularly review and adjust them as needed to stay on course.

5. **Passion and Authenticity:** Your passion for your niche and authenticity in your content are your greatest assets. Keep your audience's needs at the forefront of

your strategies.

6. **Positive Mindset:** Maintain a positive mindset and visualize your success. Believing in your potential is a powerful motivator.
7. **Balance:** Balance is key. Take breaks when necessary, prioritize self-care, and prevent burnout by managing your workload effectively.
8. **Celebrate Milestones:** Celebrate your achievements, no matter how small. These moments of recognition can boost your motivation and sense of accomplishment.

Remember that every affiliate marketer's journey is unique. What works for one may not work exactly the same for another. Embrace experimentation and adaptability as you refine your affiliate marketing strategies.

As you continue on your affiliate marketing path, keep the lessons learned and insights gained in mind. The road may be challenging at times, but with dedication, creativity, and resilience, you have the potential to achieve your affiliate marketing goals and enjoy the many rewards this field has to offer.

Your journey is just beginning, and the possibilities are boundless. So, take what you've learned, stay inspired, and embark on your affiliate marketing adventure with enthusiasm and determination. The future holds great potential for your success in the affiliate marketing landscape.